S0-EIK-392

OUR SHARED HISTORY

PUERTO RICO

From Colony to Commonwealth

Richard Worth

Enslow Publishing
101 W. 23r[illegible]
Suite 240
New York, [illegible]
USA

Published in 2016 by Enslow Publishing, LLC
101 W. 23rd Street, Suite 240, New York, NY 10011

Cataloging-in-Publication Data

Worth, Richard.
Puerto Rico: from colony to commonwealth / by Richard Worth.
p. cm. — (Our shared history)
Includes bibliographical references and index.
ISBN 978-0-7660-7004-2 (library binding)
1. Puerto Rico — History— Juvenile literature. I. Worth, Richard. II. Title.
F1971.W67 2016
972.95—d23

Printed in the United States of America

To Our Readers: We have done our best to make sure all Web Site addresses in this book were active and appropriate when we went to press. However, the author and the publisher have no control over and assume no liability for the material available on those Web sites or any Web sites they may link to. Any comments or suggestions can be sent by e-mail to customerservice@enslow.com.

Portions of this book originally appeared in the book *Puerto Rico in American History*.

Photo Credits: Alejandro O'Reilly (1722-94) (oil on canvas), Goya y Lucientes, Francisco Jose de (1746-1828)/Museo de San Telmo, San Sebastian, Spain/Bridgeman Images, p. 49; Andrew Bertino/Shutterstock.com, p. 37; © AP Images, pp. 13, 75, 93, 105, 114; ARENA Creative/Shutterstock.com (cannon throughout book); author unknown/Wikimedia Commons/Antonio Valero Bernabe.gif/public domain, p. 59; Boricuaeddie/Betances joven.gif/Wikimedia Commons/public domain, p. 7; Buyenlarge/Getty Images, p. 78; Chris Curtis/Shutterstock.com, p. 19; Chris Maddaloni/Roll Call/Getty Images, p. 108; Chris Price/E+/Getty Images, p. 34; Classic Vision/age fotostock/SuperStock, p. 62; Danita Delimont/Gallo Images/Getty Images, p. 71; DEA/G. DAGLI ORTI/De Agistini/Getty Images, p. 23; Elias H. Debbas II/Shutterstock.com, p. 28; Eric SA House - Carle/SuperStock/Getty Images, p. 14; Eugenio Caxés/Wikimedia Commons/La recuperación de la isla de Puerto Rico por el gobernador de la isla, Juan de Haro. Por Eugenio Cajés.jpg/public domain, p. 44; Francisco Oller y Cestero/Wikimedia Commons/Francisco Oller - Hacienda Aurora.jpg/public domain, p. 65; George Rose/Getty Images News/Getty Images, p. 111; Hank Walker/The LIFE Picture Collection/Getty Images, p. 96; Historic Map Works LLC/Getty Images, p. 17; Hulton Archive/Getty Images, p. 99; ilolab/Shutterstock.com (textured background throughout book); Jose Campeche y Jordan/Wikimedia Commons/Jose Campeche y Jordan - La Natividad - Google Art Project.jpg/public domain, p. 53; KPegg/Shutterstock.com, p. 37; Lauren Orr/Shutterstock.com, p. 4; Library of Congress Prints and Photographs Division, pp. 21, 43, 77, 85, 90, 94; Luis de la Cruz y Ríos (1776-1853)/Colección Yakidiro Suma, Tokio/Wikimedia Commons/DelaCruz FernandoVII.jpg/public domain, p. 57; OliverZena/Wikimedia Commons/Lares Revolutionary Flag (original).jpg/public domain, p. 11; Rawpixel/Shutterstock.com, p. 1; RDImages/Epics/Getty Images, p. 40; Space Chimp/Shutterstock.com, p. 116; T. Photography/Shutterstock.com, p. 38; Wirepec/Thinkstock.com, p. 30.

Cover Credits: Rawpixel/Shutterstock.com (Puerto Rican flags); ilolab/Shutterstock.com (textured background).

CONTENTS

The island of Puerto Rico

Chapter 1

The Lares Uprising

The small uprising began on September 23, 1868. A group of rebels, numbering about 600, attacked the town of Lares on the tiny island of Puerto Rico. Located in the western part of the island, Lares was unprepared for such a surprising attack. As a result, the invaders, wielding knives and machetes, were successful in taking over the town after a brief attack. The rebellion became known as *El Grito de Lares* (the Cry of Lares) and it was designed to liberate the island from more than three hundred years of oppressive Spanish rule.

The Origins of Rebellion

In the early sixteenth century, the Spanish settled Puerto Rico. Army generals sent from Spain served as the island's governors. A small number of Spanish immigrants, known as *peninsulares*, brought their money to the island. They established large tobacco plantations and became successful merchants. They also filled all the important political positions on the island.

By contrast, the majority of Puerto Ricans received very little from Spanish rule. These Puerto Ricans were not permitted to vote or hold government jobs. They had little money and could only afford to own small farms or shops. The Spanish did not permit freedom of speech or freedom of the press. In addition, they made Puerto Ricans pay heavy taxes to the colonial government. During the nineteenth century, the Spanish government promised to give the people of the island greater freedom. But this promise was never kept.

In 1865, the government in Spain promised again to improve conditions in Puerto Rico. The Puerto Ricans sent representatives to Madrid, the capital of Spain, to discuss a more liberal colonial policy. By 1867, the discussions in Spain had ended. The Puerto Ricans were told that new "special laws" would soon go into effect. Puerto Ricans would be able to hold positions in the colonial government and would be given the right to vote. But no such laws ever took effect. Instead, the Spanish governor began to force outspoken Puerto Rican politicians to leave the island.[1]

Among them was Ramón E. Betances. He was a physician who had started a hospital in Mayagüez, a small city in western Puerto Rico. There he had treated poor colonists who suffered from many serious diseases.

Betances fled to the Dominican Republic, located near Puerto Rico in the Caribbean. He formed the Revolutionary Committee of Puerto Rico. The committee issued the Proclamation of 1867. It stated that the colonists were "victims of the Spanish colonial system, which since Columbus has been, and will always be, the negation of every right and all justice; the absolute and irresponsible empire of a handful of greedy, inept, adventurers. . ."[2]

Ramón E. Betances is considered by many to be the father of the Puerto Rican independence movement.

Betances also issued his "Ten Commandments of Free Men" for the future of Puerto Rico. The commandments included an end to slavery and the right to vote in free elections. They also called for freedom of speech and freedom of the press.

Betances was eventually driven out of the Dominican Republic for his political views. Later he went to St. Thomas, in the Virgin Islands. The Virgin Islands are located near Puerto Rico in the Caribbean. In St. Thomas, Betances began gathering arms and ammunition for Puerto Rican rebels who sought independence. Several small groups, or cells, of rebels had already formed in the western part of Puerto Rico. The cells were located in Lares, Mayagüez, and Camuy.

The members of the revolutionary cells came from different economic groups on the island. Some rebels were small landowners. Others were peasants and farmworkers. A few were slaves. Slavery had begun in Puerto Rico during the sixteenth century. But an abolition movement, led by Betances, had demanded that the Spanish government end slavery.

All of the people involved in planning the rebellion shared a common set of beliefs. Most importantly, they wanted freedom from Spain and control over their own island. In addition, the rebels sought relief from the financial hardships they experienced under Spanish rule. Some of the small coffee growers were in debt to Spanish merchants in Puerto Rico. These merchants loaned money to the growers, but made the growers pay high interest rates. Then they bought the grower's coffee crops at low prices.[3] The rebels also complained about high taxes.

The Uprising Begins

The rebels planned to begin their attack on September 29, 1868, in Camuy. Once the revolt started, Betances was expected to land in Puerto Rico with his supplies of arms. But before the revolt could begin, the plans were discovered. Carlos Antonio Lopez, a member of the local militia, learned about the location and date of the rebellion. He also knew that the leader of the revolt was Manuel María González. González was head of the revolutionary cell in Camuy. The information was quickly relayed to the Spanish military commander in the area. His name was Colonel Manuel de Iturriaga. On September 21, in the middle of the night, Colonel Iturriaga led a small group of soldiers to Camuy. They surprised González in his home and arrested him.

When the rebels learned of the arrest, they acted quickly. The date of the rebellion was moved up to September 23. The center of the revolt was changed from Camuy to Lares. In the evening, the rebels gathered outside of Lares under the command of Manuel Rojas. He was president of the local rebel cell. Rojas carried a new flag for the Lares revolt. It had been sewed by Mariana Bracetti. The flag had two blue rectangles on the top and two red rectangles on the bottom. In the top left rectangle was a white star.

Leaving Rojas's home, the small army marched into Lares. Since they met no resistance from the local townspeople, they immediately took over the town. Along the way they had captured several Spanish merchants and burned their stores. The merchants were put behind bars in the Lares jail.

In Lares, the small army issued a proclamation. They called on "every son of this country . . . to take up arms, to help secure the freedom and independence of Puerto Rico. . ." They also selected members of a new government for an independent Puerto Rico.[4]

The next day, the rebel army planned to march to the nearby town of San Sebastián. They hoped to capture it and then move on to other communities. But the townspeople in San Sebastián knew what had happened in Lares. Most of them were loyal supporters of the Spanish government.

Rojas's army was stopped in the outskirts of San Sebastián. The local militia had taken up a strong position inside the army barracks. From there they fired on the advancing rebel army, driving them back. Rebel leaders called on the militia to join the revolt. But they refused and kept firing. An attack by the rebel army against the militia failed. As a result, the rebels retreated. Rojas wanted to advance against the militia again, but his soldiers refused. Some of his soldiers had already been killed or wounded by rifle fire.

After losing the battle near San Sebastián, the rebellion began to fall apart. The rebel army had not been supported by any towns on the island. Some Puerto Ricans were well-to-do Spanish immigrants who supported the government. Many others wanted political change but not independence from Spain. Meanwhile, Betances had been unable to sail from St. Thomas. The Spanish governor in Puerto Rico asked the authorities in St. Thomas to arrest him. Betances fled, and the arms he had collected never reached Puerto Rico.

The rebel army was not strong enough to fight the Spanish troops. They were organizing to support the

The rebel flag at El Grito de Lares

militia in San Sebastián. Spanish soldiers began rounding up people suspected of supporting the rebellion. They captured some of the military supplies hidden by the rebels. The Spanish also closed off the ports along the coast. As a result, the rebels could not flee to other islands. Many of the rebels retreated to the Puerto Rican hills and were soon arrested by the Spanish troops.

By October 1868, over five hundred men who had participated in El Grito de Lares were imprisoned. About eighty of the rebels died in jail from an epidemic of yellow fever. This is a virus carried by mosquitoes that causes high fever and sometimes death. The deaths of the rebels had an immediate effect. They prompted the Spanish governor in Puerto Rico to call off the search for any more rebel soldiers.[5]

The surviving prisoners were brought to trial, convicted, and sentenced to prison. Seven of their leaders, including Manuel Rojas, were condemned to death. But none of the death sentences was carried out. Instead the leaders of the revolt served long terms in prison.

El Grito de Lares had not achieved independence. But it had sent a message to the Spanish. Shortly after the end of the revolt, the Spanish government began freeing the slaves in Puerto Rico. New reforms went into effect. They gave the Creoles—white Puerto Ricans of Spanish descent, who had been born on the island—more political power on the island. In 1969, the date of El Grito de Lares became

El Grito de Lares Holiday

After the revolt at Lares was put down by the Spanish, the government did not allow the people of Puerto Rico to commemorate the uprising or celebrate the date as a holiday. It was not until the 1920s, after Puerto Rico became a territory of the United States, that small celebrations began at Lares. Eventually, in 1969, Lares became a national historic site designated by the Institute of Puerto Rican Culture, and it is currently known as the birthplace of Puerto Rican nationalism.

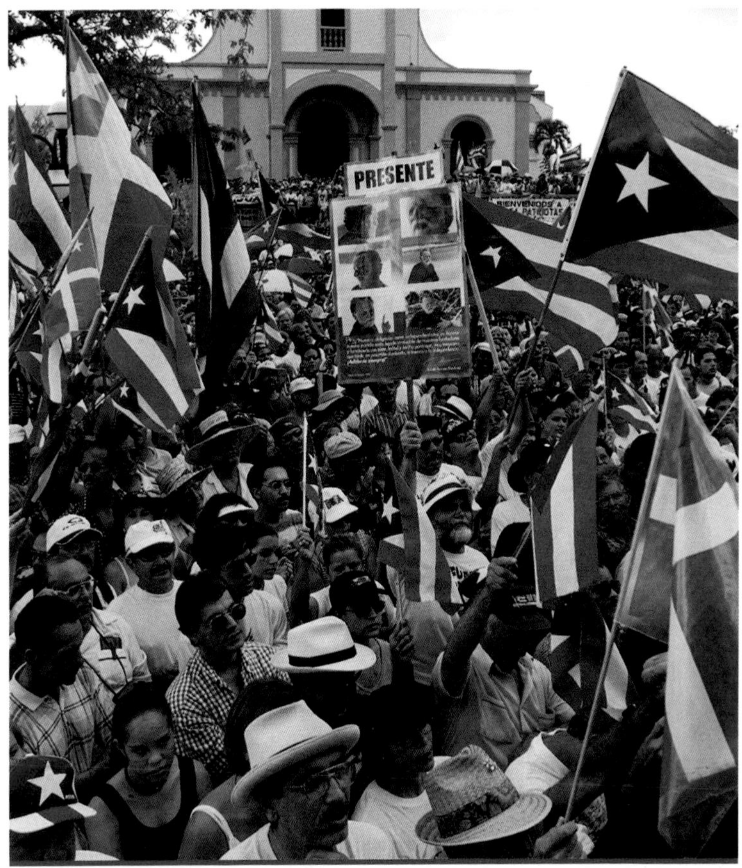

Every year in Puerto Rico, thousands gather to remember the 1868 revolt at El Grito de Lares.

a national holiday in Puerto Rico. It remains a rallying cry for many Puerto Ricans who still hope to achieve independence for their island.

Today, Puerto Rico is a commonwealth of the United States. But it has a long history that has led to this point. The first European explorers landed on the island over five hundred years ago.

Christopher Columbus landed in what he called San Juan Bautista in 1493. He claimed the island for Spain and left after only two days.

Chapter 2

A Conflict of Cultures

In November 1493, a year after he had arrived in the New World, Admiral Christopher Columbus and his squadron arrived at another island in the Caribbean Sea. Fifteen hundred settlers accompanied Columbus, who maneuvered his sailing ships along the western part of the island, weighed anchor, and ordered his crew to put down the sails. Some of them then rowed ashore in small boats, and Columbus named the newly discovered island *San Juan Bautista de Puerto Rico* (St. John the Baptist of the Rich Port). But to the Taíno Indians who inhabited the island, it was Boriquen.

"Near the landing place," according to historian R. A. Van Middeldyk, "was a deserted village consisting of a dozen huts . . . surrounding a larger one of superior construction; from the village a road or walk, hedged in by trees and plants, led to the sea . . ."[1] Columbus and his sailors saw none of the local people. Two days later, after doing some fishing, the Spanish left San Juan Bautista. They headed for the settlement that Columbus had established a year earlier. It was located on the nearby island of Hispaniola.

This was the first encounter between Europeans and the local Indian culture on the island now known as Puerto Rico.

Taíno Culture

Puerto Rico is part of a large group of islands that stretch for twenty-five hundred miles across the Caribbean. The Caribbean Sea was named after a group of people called the Carib. The islands of the Caribbean are known as the West Indies. They are located between Venezuela in South America and Florida.

Puerto Rico includes a large island and several smaller ones. The main island is hilly with lush rain forests. These rain forests were created by the warm, rainy climate in the Caribbean. The climate does not become too hot because of the trade winds blowing from the northeast. The trade winds also powered the ships led by Columbus into the Caribbean.

Before the arrival of the Spanish, Puerto Rico had been inhabited since at least the first century AD. Nomads lived on the island, hunting and fishing for food. About a century later, another group of people reached the island from South America. Archaeologists, people who study ancient civilizations, have found vases and pots made by these people. They were called the Igneri. In about the sixth century AD, another group arrived on the island from South America. They were called the Ostionoid. They built villages with ball courts outside of them. The Ostionoid also held religious ceremonies, called *areytos*, on these courts.

Puerto Rico is located in the Caribbean Sea. There are thousands of islands in the Caribbean.

Around the thirteenth century AD, the Taíno appeared in the Caribbean. They had traveled from South America. The Taíno established villages along the rivers in Puerto Rico. These villages included small round huts, called *bohios*. They were made of reeds and grass. Each bohio was large enough for several families who belonged to the same group, or clan. The Taíno decorated the inside of their bohios with wall paintings. The culture of the Taíno was called *Arawall*.

The bohios were located around a larger, rectangular-shaped house. This was the home of the *cacique*, or chief, of each village. Female chiefs were called *cacicas*. The chiefs were members of the Taíno nobility, known as *nitaínos*. The caciques, along with members of the nobility, were in charge of village life.

Each Taíno village depended on agriculture for its survival. The main crop of each village was the yucca plant. Taíno women planted yucca seeds in mounds of dirt called *montones*. When the yucca was ready for harvesting, the poisonous juices were squeezed from the roots of the plants. Then the yucca was ground into a dry meal and made into a flat bread, called cassava. In addition to yucca, the Taíno grew tobacco, corn, potatoes, and cotton. The Taíno wove the cotton into nets that they used to catch fish. They also hunted small iguanas to provide meat for their diet.

The Taíno believed that the success of their village depended on the favor of the gods. Each village had medicine men or women, called *behiques*. They healed the sick with the help of the gods and led religious ceremonies. The Taíno prayed to a supreme god, called Yocaju Bagua Maorocoti, and his mother, Atabey. The Taíno also

The Taíno people used the yucca plant, shown here, to make bread.

believed that the spirits of their dead relatives influenced events. The spirits of former chiefs were particularly powerful. They guided the caciques who succeeded them.

The caciques held the seats of honor at religious ceremonies and at ball games. These games, held at a field in the village, were played with large rubber balls. The games included as many as thirty men and women on each team. According to historian Olga Jiménez de Wagenheim, "Players could hit the ball with many parts of their bodies (head, shoulders, elbows, hips) or with a heavy ceremonial belt made of stone, but never with their hands."[2] In addition to the ball games, the Taíno enjoyed dances. They made music by beating drums hollowed out from tree trunks, gourds, and shells.

The Spanish Look for Gold

One of the men who had accompanied Columbus to San Juan Bautista in 1493 was Juan Ponce de León. Ponce de León went to Hispaniola along with the rest of the expedition. He hoped to make his fortune from the gold reportedly located on the island. But after spending a year on Hispaniola, Ponce de León probably returned to Spain. His name does not appear in the records of Hispaniola for almost a decade.

Over the next several years, the Spanish settlements on Hispaniola expanded. Much of the work building these settlements was done by the Taíno. Although the Taíno greatly outnumbered the new settlers, the Spanish had superior weapons. They brought steel swords and rifles, called *arquebuses*. The Taíno only had wooden clubs and bows and arrows. With their modern weapons, the Spanish conquered the Taíno.

The Taíno were expected to pay tribute to the Spanish. The conquerors wanted food as well as gold nuggets found in the rivers. But the Taíno's payments did not satisfy the Spanish. The conquistadors, meaning "conquerors" in Spanish, enslaved the Taíno and forced them to work on their farms. The Spanish farms were called *encomiendas*. The Spanish also forced the Taíno to work in the gold mines discovered on Hispaniola. Many Taíno died from the hard labor.

In addition, the Spanish brought new diseases with them from Europe. The Taíno had never encountered ailments like smallpox. Unlike those of the Spanish, the Taíno immune systems had not built up any defense against smallpox. As a result, thousands of Taíno and other Caribbean Indians died.

This photo shows the type of hut that was used by the Taíno.

In 1502, Ponce de León returned to Hispaniola. The island had changed. There were fewer Taíno Indians and more Spanish settlers. The Taíno resented the role that they had been forced to play on Hispaniola. In 1503, they staged a revolt against the Spanish. Ponce de León helped put down the revolt. As a reward for his services, he was given an encomienda on the eastern coast of the island. He even became mayor of a small village, Salvaleón de Higüey.

A New Spanish Settlement

Spanish ships on their way back to Spain often stopped at the eastern part of Hispaniola to pick up supplies. Then they sailed about seventy miles to San Juan Bautista. There they took on fresh water from the island's rivers before traveling across the Atlantic Ocean. The Taíno also paddled back and forth between San Juan Bautista and Hispaniola. Therefore, Ponce de León continued to hear about the island that he had visited over ten years earlier.

In 1508, Ponce de León received permission from the governor of Hispaniola, Nicolas de Ovanda, to lead an expedition to San Juan Bautista. The expedition included approximately forty or fifty sailors. With his men, Ponce de León arrived on the southern coast of the island on August 12, 1508. The Spanish met a local Taíno chief, Agüeybana I, or Agüeybana the Brave. At first there were friendly relations between the Taíno and the Spanish. The Indians entertained Ponce de León with dances and ball games. Ponce de León noticed that the chiefs wore gold disks around their necks. He was permitted to travel around the island. Agüeybana even showed him some of the streams where there were gold nuggets.[3]

At a bay where San Juan, Puerto Rico, is currently located, the Spanish established a small settlement. Ponce

The Spanish settlers forced the native people of Puerto Rico to work on their farms. The woman shown here is a slave.

de León named it Caparra. The new settlement was also known as Puerto Rico. As Ponce de León wrote:

> I built a medium-sized house with its terrace, and railing, and tall battlements, and barricade before the gate, all metal within and without . . . I had a crew gather some gold, but could not get more since . . . none of the Indians of this island would help me.[4]

Ponce de León then returned to Hispaniola. He wanted to arrange for a larger settlement on the island of Puerto Rico.

In Hispaniola, Ponce de León sent the gold from Puerto Rico back to Spain. The small treasure impressed the Spanish king, Ferdinand I. "Be very diligent in searching for gold mines in the island of San Juan," he wrote Ponce de León. "Take out as much as possible, and after smelting it [melting it down into bars] in la Espanola, send it immediately."[5] As a reward, the king named Ponce de Leon lieutenant governor of the new settlement.

Meanwhile, deposits of gold continued to be discovered on San Juan. According to historian Olga Jiménez de Wagenheim, one hundred thousand pesos of gold had been processed in the smelter by October 1510. "One fifth of this sum was sent to the King, two-fifths were assigned to cover the costs of colonization, including the expansion and fortification of the governor's house, and the remaining two-fifths were presumably kept by the miners."[6]

The Taíno Attack the Spanish Settlers

The Taíno were forced to work harder and harder to dig more gold on the island. The Spanish enslaved Taíno as well as Carib Indians, who were brought from other islands. Under the leadership of chief Agüeybana the Brave, the Taíno planned a revolt.

Some of the chiefs were afraid that they could not defeat the Spanish. The Spanish possessed superior weapons, and many of the Taíno believed that they were gods who could not be killed. But at least one chief, Urayoan, was not convinced of their immortality. Urayoan ordered his men to conduct an experiment to find out if the Spanish were indeed gods. A Spaniard, named Salcedo, had asked several Taíno to carry him across a deep river. As they reached the middle, the Indians dropped Salcedo. They held him under the water until he drowned. Then they brought him to shore to find out if he would come back to life. But Salcedo remained dead. Therefore, the Taíno were convinced that the Spanish were not immortal.

Repartimientos

The leading members of the Spanish settlement received Taíno Indians as slaves, a process called a *repartimiento*, a Spanish word that means "distribution." The Spanish settlers did not expect to plant and harvest crops themselves, but expected the Taíno slaves to do it for them. The commander of the new colony, Ponce de León, acquired two hundred Indians, beginning in 1509. Another well-to-do Spaniard, Christóbal Sotomayor, was given one hundred Taíno. Vicente Yáñez Pinzón, who also accompanied Ponce de León, received one hundred Indians, "on condition that he should settle in the island." In all, over one thousand Taíno were assigned to leading Spanish settlers on San Juan.[7]

A Struggle for Power

When Ponce de León was named lieutenant governor of the island in 1509, he did not remain in his new position for very long. Diego Columbus, the son of Christopher Columbus, decided to replace Ponce de León. Diego Columbus claimed that he should have the authority to select all the governors of islands that had been visited by his father. Columbus wanted his friend Juan Ceron named as lieutenant governor. Ceron became lieutenant governor in October 1509. But a few months later, Diego Columbus was ordered by King Ferdinand to replace Ceron with Ponce de León. Finally, in 1511, Ceron returned and became governor of the territory.

Early in 1511, the Taíno chiefs met to launch a revolt. The Taíno ambushed Christóbal Sotomayor and his men, killing almost all of them. Then they set fire to his settlement, taking the lives of eighty settlers. One of Sotomayor's men escaped and brought word of the revolt to Ponce de León at Caparra. Ponce de León gathered together ninety men and split them into three groups. He left one to defend Caparra and brought the others with him.

Ponce de León learned that the main body of Taíno warriors, about eleven thousand men, was gathered in

Yaguecas. He rapidly approached the Indian army. Before beginning the battle, Ponce de León built a fortified encampment to protect his men. From this position, his riflemen, called arquebusiers, advanced through the woods toward the Taíno. They began firing at the Indians, killing many of them. Eventually, Ponce de León ordered one of his men to aim for the Taíno leader, Agüeybana. With a single shot, Agüeybana was killed. Without a leader, the Taíno army began to fall apart. Some of them eventually surrendered to the Spanish.

But many of the Taíno hid in the forests of San Juan. Others escaped to the small islands off the coast. From their hideouts, they continued to mount hit-and-run attacks. These continued against the Spanish for many years afterward. The Taíno were joined by the Carib. They invaded Puerto Rico from other Caribbean islands, such as Guadeloupe and Dominica. As battles continued, the population of the Taíno declined. There had been an estimated sixty thousand Indians on the island in 1509. Only about fourteen thousand five hundred remained in 1515.[8] Many died of disease or overwork in the mines and on the encomiendas. By the end of the sixteenth century, the Taíno had almost disappeared.[9]

The Spanish Colony Expands

Meanwhile, the Spanish increased their control of the island. A new settlement was founded at San German, on the western part of the island. The settlers led campaigns from San German against the Taíno and the Carib. Ponce de León continued to play an important role on the island. He helped to defend San Juan Bautista from attacks by the Taíno. King Ferdinand also requested that Ponce de León establish two town governments on the island. These were

A statue of Ponce de León stands in Plaza San Jose in Old San Juan, Puerto Rico.

known as cabildos. One cabildo in Caparra had authority in the eastern part of the island. The other cabildo in San German had authority over the western region.

Even with these responsibilities, Ponce de León found life on San Juan too settled. In 1515, he led an expedition north to explore an area that he called La Florida. Thus, he became the first Spaniard to reach Florida. In 1521, the explorer returned to Florida where he was wounded by a poisoned arrow in a battle with Calusa Indians. Ponce de León died before ever returning to San Juan. Two years later, the Spanish moved Caparra from one side of the bay to an island in the bay itself. They also changed the name of the settlement to San Juan. Meanwhile, the entire island became known as Puerto Rico.

Few settlers came to the island of Puerto Rico in its early years as a Spanish colony.

Chapter 3

The Spanish Government

At first, the tiny island of Puerto Rico remained an insignificant part of the Spanish empire. The colony struggled to survive economically and the population grew slowly, reaching only about 400 by 1530.[1] The life of the colonists was never easy, as they had to battle heavy storms, ambushes by the local Indians, a struggling economy, and invasion from abroad.

Indian attacks continued throughout the 1500s. In 1529, the Carib sailed eight large canoes into San Juan harbor. The town's defense was led by Governor Antonio de La Gama. He was Ponce de León's son-in-law. The colonists fired at the Carib. But the Carib still managed to kill several people before retreating. A larger attack occurred in 1530, when five hundred Carib struck the gold mines of Llaguello. They killed a well-to-do landowner named Christopher Guzman. The Carib also killed many other Puerto Rican settlers and burned their homes. The colonists eventually launched expeditions against the Carib during the 1530s. They burned Carib homes on neighboring islands and imprisoned some Carib women and children.[2]

While the colonists dealt with Indian attacks, they also had to cope with natural disasters. The island of Puerto Rico is located in the path of giant storms called hurricanes. The storms sweep through the Caribbean during the summer and fall. During a period of six weeks in July and August 1530, three hurricanes struck the island. One of the colonists wrote:

> The storms have destroyed all the plantations, drowned many cattle, and caused a great dearth [shortage] of food. Half of the houses in this city [San Juan] have been blown down; of the other half those that are least damaged are without roofs. In the country and at the mines not a house is left standing. Everybody has been impoverished and thinking of going away.[3]

Resources of the Island

The hurricanes as well as the Indian attacks made a heavy impact on the island. These disasters convinced some colonists that they might be better off living somewhere else in the Spanish empire. By the 1530s, Spain had conquered Mexico and a large part of South America. Peru, located in South America, had been ruled by the Inca Indians. Spanish conquistadors defeated the Incas and captured a large treasure in gold and silver. News of this treasure reached Puerto Rico by 1534. Some colonists decided to leave the island for Peru. Governor Francisco Manuel de Lando resorted to harsh punishments to prevent more colonists from leaving. In a letter to the Spanish king, he wrote, "I have imposed the death penalty on whoever shall attempt to leave the island."[4]

Meanwhile, the mines in Puerto Rico were producing less gold. Production had fallen by more than two thirds.[5] Miners had begun importing African slaves to dig deeper into the mines for new gold deposits. Some of the slaves were purchased from other Spanish colonies in the Caribbean. Others were shipped directly from West Africa. By the 1530s, more than two thousand slaves lived in Puerto Rico.[6]

Eventually the mines ran out of gold, and some miners left Puerto Rico. Governor Lando wrote the Spanish government that it must invest money into the island's economy to prevent more people from leaving. Some settlers had already begun to grow sugarcane on the island. In the warm, humid climate, sugarcane flourished. Once the cane was harvested, it was taken to mills. There the juice was pressed from the cane and turned into sugar. The sugar was exported to Spain. The mills were expensive to build, and Governor Lando persuaded the Spanish government to loan money to the colony. By 1550, ten mills were operating on the island.[7] The settlers were also importing more slaves to work in the sugarcane fields.

At first, sugarcane seemed to offer a solution to the island's economic struggles. But Puerto Rican sugarcane had to compete against cane grown in Spain. The Puerto Rican sugar planters were also required to ship the sugar back to Spain on Spanish ships. But very few ships came to Puerto Rico each year. Most of them went to Mexico or South America in order to transport gold and silver back to Spain. The Spanish government also did not send a sufficient number of African slaves to work in the Puerto Rican

These workers are harvesting sugarcane, which was an important crop in the 1500s.

cane fields to make large profits. As a result, the sugarcane industry declined.

During the sixteenth and seventeenth centuries, the colonists replaced sugarcane with other crops. These included ginger, tobacco, and cocoa. Tobacco became very important on the island. As one colonist said, "The use of tobacco is such that it prevails over the necessity of eating."[8] In addition, the colonists raised large herds of cattle. The cattle were slaughtered for food, and the cattle hides were turned into leather for shoes and clothing.

Many colonists did not sell their crops directly to Spain. They found they could get more in return for the goods in the Caribbean, so they began smuggling, or secretly selling, goods to other islands. By the 1600s, England, Holland, and France had established colonies on some of the Caribbean islands. There was very little cash in the islands. Therefore, according to historian Arturo Morales Carrion, most of the trade was "conducted by barter: local goods [from Puerto Rico] . . . hides, tobacco, livestock, ginger, and wood were traded for slaves, wheat, clothes, agricultural implements, tools, household utensils, and other basic supplies."[9] Spain brought very few of these supplies to Puerto Rico. Instead, they were shipped to South America and Mexico.

Smuggling was illegal. If the Puerto Rican smugglers were caught, they could receive stiff prison sentences. They might even be executed by the Spanish government. But many colonists continued to smuggle goods off the island. Much of the smuggling occurred outside of San Juan, the main port. Towns such as Aguado and Arecibo sprung up along the coast. There, merchants carried on a brisk smuggling business. Many colonial officials knew about the smuggling, but they did little to stop it. According to

Carrion, "Political, administrative, and military authorities . . . and even the island's governors, were involved."[10] Smuggling helped them increase their incomes. They were often poorly paid by the Spanish government.[11]

The Spanish Military Occupation

The Spanish government regarded Puerto Rico as a presidio. That means it was an important military post in the Caribbean empire. Known as the "key to the Indies," the island was often the first stop for Spanish ships sailing from Spain to South America.[12] The Spanish considered Puerto Rico and the Spanish colony of Cuba to be the first line of defense for their other colonies. During the 1530s, Spain began constructing a fort in San Juan. It was known as La Fortaleza. Construction of the fort was completed in 1540. But no cannon arrived to defend the fort until fifteen years later.

Meanwhile, the Spanish began erecting walls around San Juan for protection. During the 1540s, work also began on a massive fort called El Morro. It was located on a rocky piece of land overlooking San Juan harbor. Work on El Morro continued for many years. The Spanish government sent cannons to protect the fort and increased the number of troops from fifty to over two hundred. The cost of building El Morro was financed from a special fund known as the situado. The situado was shipped to Puerto Rico from the silver deposits in Mexico.

While the Spanish improved the fortifications in San Juan, other parts of the island were largely neglected. As a result, they were open to attack by French and English sea captains. The sea captains wanted to take Puerto Rico for their own governments. San German, for example, was struck repeatedly by the French.

El Morro was built by the Spanish in the sixteenth century. The fort survived many attacks by foreign forces.

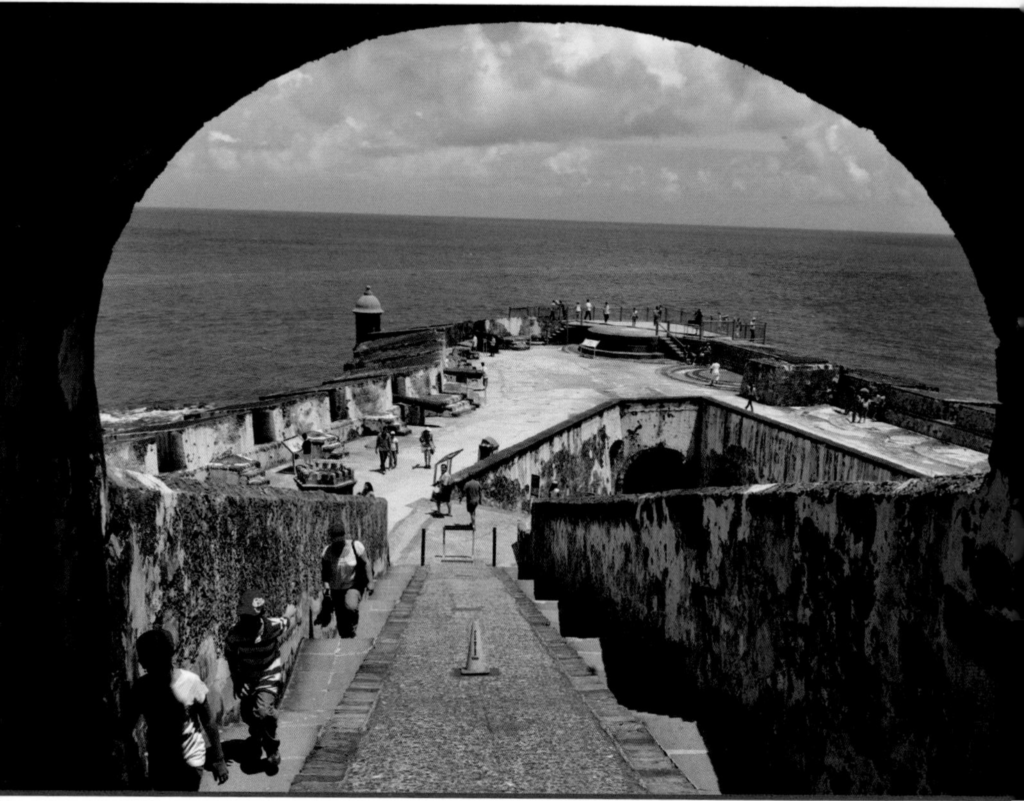

El Morro was built to defend the harbor at San Juan. Tourists can explore its dungeons and secret tunnels.

In 1595, a squadron of twenty-seven English ships mounted a major attack against Puerto Rico. The attack was led by Sir Francis Drake. Several years earlier, in 1588, Drake had led the English navy in its defeat of the Spanish Armada. This was a large fleet of Spanish ships that intended to invade England. The invasion was part of a lengthy war between Spain and England for control of the seas. During the war, Drake had attacked Spanish colonies and captured Spanish treasure ships.

Before Drake arrived, a crippled Spanish ship arrived in the harbor at San Juan. General Sancho Pardo y Osorio, the ship's commander, carried a huge treasure of gold and silver. Twice a year, the Spanish sent a treasure fleet from the New World—which included North and South America and the West Indies—back to Spain. The treasure was transferred to San Juan for safe keeping. It remained there until the rest of the fleet arrived, including several Spanish frigates that had recently engaged in a battle with English ships. The Spanish had learned that Drake's fleet was sailing for Puerto Rico.

On November 22, 1595, Drake's fleet appeared off San Juan. The Spanish had sunk two ships in the harbor to prevent Drake's fleet from entering. If Drake tried to sail over them, the bottom of his ships would scrape the sunken vessels, spring holes, and sink. Once night fell, Drake sent out twenty-five small boats filled with sailors to enter the harbor. Their mission was to burn the Spanish frigates. As several of the Spanish ships caught on fire, the English boats were revealed. Spanish gunners at El Morro began firing on the English. Drake's losses amounted to about four hundred seamen. Soon afterward, he called off his attack and sailed away from the island.

In 1598, the English launched another attack on San Juan. Begun in June, the attacking troops were led by Lord George Cumberland. They landed outside the city and marched inland. Most of the residents had fled from San Juan, which was captured. Nevertheless, Spanish troops defended El Morro with about four hundred soldiers. They were under the command of Governor Antonio Mosquera. However, the Spanish were short of food and ammunition.

Sir Francis Drake and the English navy tried unsuccessfully to attack Puerto Rico.

They surrendered El Morro to the English after a siege of fifteen days.

As a result of their victory, the English hoped to take control of Puerto Rico. But they were struck by an epidemic of yellow fever. Many soldiers died, and the English left the island in September.

Following these attacks, the Spanish improved the defenses of El Morro. During the seventeenth century, they added more guns and ammunition. In 1625, San Juan withstood another attack. This one was mounted

A Letter from the Dutch

Dutch leader Balduino Enrico sent a letter to Governor de Haro. He threatened to burn San Juan unless the Spanish surrendered El Morro. In reply, the governor wrote:

> **...the settlers have enough courage to rebuild their houses, for there is timber in the mountains and building materials in the land. And here I am today with people enough in this fortress to wipe out yours; and do not write any more such letters for I will not reply; and this is what I choose to answer. And concerning the rest, do as you please.[13]**

by the Dutch under the command of Balduino Enrico. With a fleet of eight ships, Enrico sailed into the harbor and landed his troops in San Juan before laying siege to El Morro. His troops dug trenches around the fortress. Enrico then demanded the surrender of El Morro's commanding officer, Governor Juan de Haro. But Governor de Haro refused.

Protecting the Spanish Colonies

As a way of protecting its colonies in the New World, Spain established the *Guarda Costas* (Coast Guard). These were independent Spanish sea captains, or privateers. One of their responsibilities was to stop smuggling by colonial traders. They were also expected to approach any foreign vessel on a "suspicious course." The privateers escorted the vessel into a Spanish port, where its cargo was inspected. The port authorities then paid the privateers for their services.

Among the best known privateers was Miguel Henriquez, a shoemaker from Puerto Rico. He was of African descent. By the early eighteenth century, he was considered the most powerful member of the Guarda Costas in the Caribbean.[14]

This engraving from 1671 shows the harbor of San Juan, Puerto Rico.

Instead, the governor ordered attacks against the Dutch manning the trenches. One attack on October 5, led by Captain Juan de Amezquita, killed sixty Dutch soldiers.[15] Since the Dutch could not capture El Morro, they decided to burn San Juan. They set fire to the city on October 22 and then sailed away. The settlers returned to San Juan and rebuilt the port. During the seventeenth century, the city was enclosed behind thick stone walls and towers that provided protection against future attacks.

Religion and Politics

Governors like Juan de Haro were the leading political figures in Puerto Rico. They were appointed by the Spanish king for a term of two to five years. Most of the governors

Juan de Haro, left, was governor of Puerto Rico from 1625 to 1630.

were soldiers. In fact, they were also given the title of captain-general—that is, leader of the colonial armed forces. Defending the colony was the most important responsibility of every governor. But he had other duties as well, like collecting taxes and preventing smuggling.

The governor was also involved in local government. He appointed the *regidores*, or aldermen, of the *cabildos*, which ran San Juan and San German. They were appointed from the leading members of the colony, like the few large cattle ranchers and the men who ran *haciendas*, or large estates. Cabildos insured that local farmers supplied enough beef and flour to the towns to feed their inhabitants. This was called the *abasto publico* (public supply). The beef and flour were sold at prices determined by the cabildos. Nevertheless, farmers regularly tried to ignore the abasto. They smuggled their produce to other islands for higher prices.

In addition to the abasto, the cabildos also sold public lands to settlers. The money from these sales was used to maintain the cleanliness of the local slaughterhouses, where beef was prepared. Much of the land was settled by peasant farmers known as *jibaros*. They lived in the interior of the island, usually in small huts. The jibaros grew corn and other food crops on a few acres of land.

Outside the government, the Catholic Church had important responsibilities in the colony, especially in converting the local Indians to Christianity. The Dominicans, an order of Catholic priests, had urged the Spanish authorities to treat the Taíno humanely. The Ordinances of Valladolid were passed in 1513 regarding the treatment of the Indians. The Taíno on the encomiendas were supposed to be given wooden houses. They were to be supplied with food and clothing. They were also not expected to do extremely heavy work. In addition, each Indian baby was supposed to be baptized as a Christian. Children were expected to be taught the elements of the Catholic faith. Most of these rules were violated, however, by the landowners.

Nevertheless, the Dominicans continued to speak out against the harsh treatment of the Indians in Puerto Rico. Dominicans, as well as another order of monks called Franciscans, built churches in San Juan and San German. Monks were among the few people educated to read and write. Therefore, they served as teachers in the colony. Some taught the Taíno, while others opened schools for the colonists. The monks opened schools in San Juan during the seventeenth century. One of them, founded by Bishop Francisco Padilla, was free to poor children.

By the end of the seventeenth century, the colonial population of the island had grown. The Spanish paid for new colonists to travel to the New World from Europe. Four hundred families arrived in Puerto Rico during the 1680s and 1690s. But the number of settlers by 1700 was still small—only about six thousand.[16] They would face stiff, new challenges in the years ahead.

Chapter 4

Colonial Growth and Development

Over the next two centuries, Puerto Rico remained quite small. In 1765, the Spanish authorities conducted a census of the island and found that a mere forty-four thousand people lived there. By contrast, British North America contained one million settlers. To learn more about conditions on the island, the government in Spain sent one of its leading military men, Marshall Alejandro O'Reilly, to visit Puerto Rico and report back on conditions there. Born in Ireland, O'Reilly had distinguished himself during a long career in the Spanish army.

In his report to the Spanish government, Marshall O'Reilly called the Puerto Rican people "the poorest that there are in [the Spanish Empire in] America." He commented that the island had no roads. The Puerto Rican government did not produce its own money to encourage business. Many people supported themselves by smuggling. Finally, the local government had to support itself on the situado that came from Mexico.[1] As O'Reilly put it:

> In all the island, there are only two schools for children . . . few know how to read. They count time by . . . hurricanes, visits of the Bishop, arrivals of ships, or of funds from Mexico. . . All of the towns, except for Puerto Rico [San Juan], have no more permanent population than that of the priest. The others are always in the countryside, except on Sundays, when those near the church come to mass. . . .[2]

Marshall O'Reilly made several important recommendations. First, he suggested that the island be permitted to trade with other areas in addition to Spain. O'Reilly noted that much of the colony's economy depended on smuggling. The islanders smuggled out goods like timber, animal hides, and tobacco. Soon afterward, the Spanish government permitted the islanders to begin trading with other Spanish colonies in the Caribbean. Over the next three decades, trade expanded to ports in North America. From the mainland of North America, English colonists began shipping flour to Puerto Rico.

Spain's financial resources were declining as a result of many wars in Europe. In addition, the mines in South America were running out of gold and silver. Because Spain was short of funds to support its colonies, the Spanish government permitted merchants from North America to increase their trade with Puerto Rico. In turn, Puerto Rican colonists traded sugar with the United States.

Marshall O'Reilly also reformed the colony's military operations. He recognized that the troops were poorly paid. Often the situado to pay them arrived months behind schedule. In addition, some of the officers were

Marshall Alejandro O'Reilly worked to improve Puerto Rico's military.

corrupt. O'Reilly removed them from command. O'Reilly also upgraded the training of the Spanish troops and the colonial militia. For this work, he was called the "father of the Puerto Rican militia." Finally, he urged the Spanish government to strengthen the fortifications around San Juan.

As a result of O'Reilly's recommendations, pay was more than doubled for Spanish officers assigned to Puerto Rico. The forts around San Juan were also reinforced. These improvements enabled the islanders to defend themselves when the English attacked the island in 1797.

The English were under the command of Sir Ralph Abercromby. His force included a flotilla of sixty English frigates and seven thousand soldiers. They anchored off the island on April 17. As they approached El Morro, however, the British were driven back by heavy fire from the guns in the forts. When the British tried to land outside of San Juan, they were attacked by Spanish troops and militia. The defenders were commanded by Governor Ramón de Castro, who drove off the British attack. During the summer, British troops tried to land on other parts of the island. But the colonial militia succeeded in driving them back to their ships. Eventually the British flotilla left the island and never attacked Puerto Rico again.

Puerto Rican Settlements in the 18th Century

During the eighteenth century, more and more towns sprung up on the island. These included communities along the coast, like Ponce and Mayagüez. By the last half of the eighteenth century, San German and San Juan were still the largest communities. But Ponce had over three thousand settlers, and Guayama about twenty-five hundred.[3]

At the top of the social pyramid in the capital, San Juan, were the Spaniards. These included government officials, like Governor de Castro, and commanders of the Spanish garrisons. There were also a few *hacendados*, or hacienda owners, and cattle ranchers. Some of them were Creoles. These were white Puerto Ricans of Spanish descent who had been born on the island. They occupied the next rung on the social ladder.

The well-to-do Spanish and Creoles lived in spacious brick homes. The homes were built around quiet court-yards, planted with beautiful gardens. For recreation, they enjoyed gambling, horse racing, and dancing. In fact, most Puerto Ricans enjoyed going to a dance. As Father Iñigo Abbad y Lasierra wrote:

> When someone gives a dance, the news travels throughout the territory. . . . Since the houses are small, most guests stay outside until they wish to dance. To begin the dance, the guests stand at the foot of the stairs with their . . . small guitars; and sing a song honoring the owner of the house. . . . The women sit on benches or hammocks; the men remain standing, or crouch down upon their heels. . . . They come out to dance one by one, or two by two . . ."[4]

Some of the hacendados were immigrants from the Canary Islands. Others came from the island of Haiti. During the 1790s, a slave revolt had broken out on that island. The French government and the wealthy plantation owners were driven out. The former slaves established a republic. Many of the French fled to Puerto Rico where they set up new coffee or sugar plantations. The hacendados lived in large houses built on stilts. They had wide porches to take advantage of the breezes that blew across the island.

The world of the wealthy hacendados was far different from that of the poor who worked on the large estates. They lived in small huts made of wood, with thatched roofs. These poor workers were known as *agregados*,

Puerto Rican Artist, José Campeche

Some wealthy people could afford paintings by the colony's best-known artist, José Campeche. He was born in 1752. His mother was white Hispanic and his father was a freed slave of African descent. Therefore, Campeche was a person of mixed race. Campeche painted landscapes. He also created religious paintings for the churches on the island and portraits of the wealthy. Among his best-known paintings is a portrait of Governor Miguel Antonio De Ustariz, who served from 1789 to 1792.

Campeche's religion-themed paintings include *La Natividad*. He painted many pictures of the Virgin Mary and Jesus Christ as a child. Not only was Campeche a talented artist, but he also taught his brothers and his sister to paint. José Campeche died in 1809.

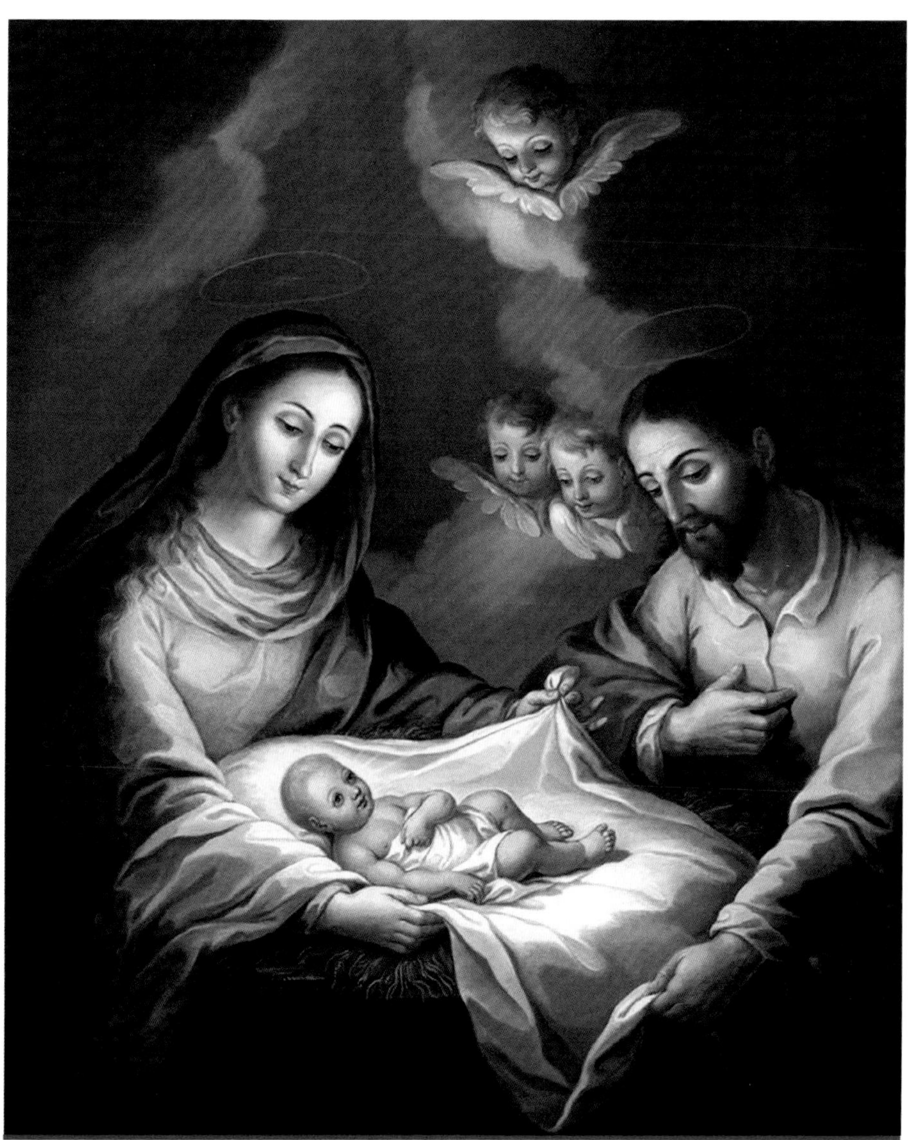

José Campeche was the most famous Puerto Rican artist of the late eighteenth century. He was known for his religious paintings, like *La Natividad*, shown here.

or squatters. They cultivated a small plot of land on the hacienda. In return, they gave part of their crop to the hacendados. In addition to the agregados, slaves lived on the haciendas. They did most of the work. As sugar and coffee production grew, the number of slaves increased. The slave population was about five thousand in 1765. By the end of the century, the number of slaves had increased to over thirteen thousand.[5]

Some of the slaves worked inside the homes of the hacendados. Others worked in the sugarcane fields. They planted, weeded, and harvested the cane. Then they cut the cane stalks and brought them to the sugar mills.

In addition to slaves, Puerto Rico also had a large number of free blacks. By the beginning of the nineteenth century, an estimated 60 percent of blacks and mulattoes—people of mixed race—in Puerto Rico were free. Since the seventeenth century, Puerto Rico offered freedom to any slaves escaping from Caribbean islands controlled by other nations.[6] This was an effort to attract new settlers to the island. In addition, some Puerto Rican slaves were freed after their masters died. Freedom was granted by their masters' wills.

Changes During the Nineteenth Century

During the early nineteenth century, many settlers on the island began to enjoy greater freedom. This change occurred as a result of events in Europe. Since the beginning of the century, France had been ruled by Emperor Napoléon Bonaparte. Under Bonaparte's leadership, French armies took control of large areas in western Europe. In 1808, Napoléon invaded Spain. French troops drove out the Spanish king, Ferdinand VII. Napoléon placed his own brother, Joseph, on the Spanish throne.

Many Spanish political leaders, however, remained loyal to King Ferdinand. They formed a new government in northern Spain to oppose the French.

In Spain's empire in the New World, the colonists felt no loyalty to the new French government. The Creoles decided that the time had come to establish their own governments. Revolutions broke out across Latin America. They were led by General Simón Bolívar. By the 1820s, Spain had lost its empire. The former colonies had become independent republics.

In Puerto Rico, events followed a different path. There were fewer Creoles, and most of them did not want independence. The colony also had a large military force that could put down a revolt. Nevertheless, the Creoles did demand greater political power on the island. In Spain, the Spanish government that remained loyal to Ferdinand decided to give Puerto Rico more authority. The government invited the Puerto Ricans to send a delegate to the Spanish parliament, called the *Cortes*. Never before had the Spanish colonies been given any representation in Spain.

In Puerto Rico, Governor Toribio Montes called on the cabildos to select candidates for Puerto Rico's representative to the Cortes. From the list of candidates, he selected Ramón Power y Giralt. Born in 1775 in San Juan, Power y Giralt was a well-to-do Creole. He was educated in Spain and later joined the Spanish navy. Eventually, he became an admiral. In 1810, Power y Giralt journeyed to Cadiz, Spain. He carried ideas with him from the cabildos that were designed to change the government of Puerto Rico.

The key change was ending what the cabildos called "oppressive, arbitrary, and tyrannical" rule by the Spanish.[7] Their rule prevented freedom of the press in Puerto Rico.

It also kept Creoles like Power y Giralt from serving in the colonial government. The cabildos wanted the Spanish to stop sending out all exports through the single port of San Juan. They urged the government to allow other coastal communities to participate in the trade.

Power y Giralt presented his ideas to the Cortes. Between 1811 and 1812, the Cortes approved the Ley Power (Power Act). This law enabled other communities in Puerto Rico to legally export goods from the island. An intendant, Alejandro Ramirez, was appointed to take charge of the colony's financial affairs. Puerto Rico had lost a large amount of revenue because the situado had ended. Ramirez changed the tax program. He also began a state lottery system to improve revenues. The colony continued to have a representative in the Cortes. The Creoles were given positions in the colonial government. In addition, colonists were permitted to speak openly about political issues.

Power y Giralt died in Cadiz in 1813, from yellow fever. A year later, the French were driven out of Spain. Ferdinand VII returned to power and immediately tore up the new laws passed by the Cortes. The Cortes was abolished. The king also tried to retake the colonies in Latin America that had revolted from Spanish rule. Puerto Rico became an important military base for the Spanish. From the island, they launched attacks against the rebels in South America.

Another period of liberal government occurred in Spain from 1820 to 1823. The army in Spain revolted and forced Ferdinand to adopt a more liberal constitution. This brought immediate changes to Puerto Rico. The Creoles were given increased political freedom again, much as

King Ferdinand VII ruled Spain in 1808 and then again from 1814 to 1833. At first, he accepted the restored liberal constitution of 1812, but once he regained his power, he reestablished the absolute monarchy.

they had been in 1812. But in 1823, Ferdinand regained his power and ended that political freedom. A Spanish dictatorship returned to Puerto Rico and lasted until the 1860s.

Ferdinand clamped down on the political rights of the Puerto Ricans. Yet he still recognized that the support of the islanders was important to the future of the Spanish empire. Therefore, he encouraged the Puerto Rican cabildos to recommend economic changes that would lead to the growth of the colony. This resulted in the *Cedula de Gracias* (Decree of Graces).

Under the terms of the Cedula de Gracias, immigrants were encouraged to come to the island. New immigrants were given free land in Puerto Rico to build their homes and develop farms. They were also permitted to avoid paying any taxes to the government. These included sales taxes and slave taxes for each slave they owned. Trade regulations were also improved. Trade with Spain was free of any taxes. Trade with other Spanish colonies in the Western Hemisphere was taxed at only a 2 percent rate. In addition, trade with North America was taxed at only 6 percent.[8] In part because of the Cedula de Gracias, the population grew by almost 40 percent over the next twenty years.[9]

The Cedula de Gracias also encouraged the growth of the Puerto Rican economy. New immigrants opened stores in various towns like Ponce and Mayagüez. They imported goods from abroad. In addition, they grew tobacco, sugar, coffee, and other items to sell in the United States. The United States became the primary market for Puerto Rican sugar. Approximately three quarters of the sugar produced on the island was sold to the United States during the 1830s.

Antonio Valero de Bernabé

Antonio Valero de Bernabé was born in Puerto Rico in 1790. He believed that the island colony should try to achieve independence. After being educated in Spain, Valero de Bernabé joined the Spanish army. He participated in the battles that eventually drove the French out of the Spanish peninsula.

When Ferdinand VII decided not to abide by the laws passed in the Cortes, Valero de Bernabé left Spain. He went to Mexico and fought in the independence movement against the Spanish government. Later he joined Simón Bolívar in the struggle to free the Spanish colonies in South America. During the 1820s, Valero de Bernabé also planned to invade Puerto Rico. He wanted to set the island free. But this invasion never occurred. Valero de Bernabé later returned to Colombia where he died in 1863.

Antonio Valero de Bernabé

Much of the sugar was produced in Ponce, Guayama, and Mayagüez.[10]

Slavery in Puerto Rico

The coffee and sugar hacendados relied on slaves to do the difficult work of growing and harvesting the crops. According to historian James Dietz, slaves made up only about 11 percent of the Puerto Rican population. This was far less than on any other island in the Caribbean. Nevertheless, as Dietz points out, the figure is misleading. In heavy sugar-growing areas like Mayagüez and Ponce, there were many more slaves. They numbered between 20 and 30 percent of the population. Their percentage of the labor force—working adults—was even higher. In Ponce, slaves numbered more than 80 percent of the labor force in 1845.[11]

The treatment of slaves was governed by a slave code. The code was developed by the Spanish governor in 1826. It required owners to limit the normal workday to no more than nine hours. Slaves were supposed to be fed three times a day by their owners. In addition, any disobedience by a slave was not to be treated with harsh or inhuman punishments. Unfortunately, no courts in Puerto Rico protected the rights of the slaves. Therefore, masters were not brought into court if they violated the laws.

Balanced against the humane aspects of the code were other harsher elements. Some slaves traveled from one hacienda to another. They were hired out by the hacendados, who received payment for their work. These slaves were not permitted to travel without written passes. Slaves were also required to be locked in their rooms at night. In addition, any tools that they used were to be taken away

An Account of Slavery

Slaves were transported to Puerto Rico from Africa. George Coggeshall visited the island in the nineteenth century. He described a slave ship bringing its cargo to Puerto Rico. There were approximately five hundred slaves aboard the ship.

> I saw the remnant of these cargoes for sale in three enclosures. . . . There was a little stream of fresh water near where these slaves were kept, and in this little river they were made to bathe daily; if they showed any reluctance to go into the water they were driven in like cattle. They had some rude instruments of music, such as banjoes . . . on these instruments they were encouraged to play, singing and dancing at the same time to keep up their spirits. The vendors of these negroes told me it was absolutely necessary to keep them in a good-natured mood, otherwise they would . . . refuse all kind of food, and die with starvation.

Coggeshall reported that children were being sold for about one hundred dollars each. Slave traders charged two hundred fifty to three hundred dollars for adults.[12]

Juan González de la Pezuela y Ceballos was the governor of Puerto Rico from 1848 to 1851. His libreta law gave officials the power to track how many hours the jornaleros worked.

from them. These measures were designed to prevent slaves from organizing revolts.

Despite these precautions, fourteen slave revolts occurred in Puerto Rico between 1795 and 1848. Slaves attacked their owners and burned sugarcane fields. To prevent revolts, slaves were encouraged to report possible uprisings. They were offered a reward and their freedom for informing the authorities. In addition to revolts, slaves regularly escaped from their masters.[13] While some were caught, others managed to hide in the Puerto Rican highlands. There they established communities with other former slaves.

By the 1840s, the slave population had risen to over fifty-one thousand. Still, there were not enough slaves to do all the work required on the haciendas. The hacendados wanted to control the *jornaleros*, who were hired workers. They wanted to force the jornaleros to do more work on the haciendas. As a result, Puerto Rican governors issued laws to force the jornaleros to work longer hours. Many hacendados accused the jornaleros of laziness. According to a local newspaper, the jornaleros only worked a few days at a time. They "regularly left work at noontime and often failed to appear at all, because they found two or three days of work to be sufficient." They did not need more money to buy food. The rest of their needs could be filled from food growing wild on the island. This food included fruit and plantains, which are similar to bananas.[14]

In 1849 Governor Juan de la Pezuela issued the so-called *libreta* law. Jornaleros were forced to carry a libreta, or workbook. An employer took the libreta when the jornaleros went to work. Then the employer wrote down how many days the jornaleros had actually been on the job. The entries in the libretas also included the jornaleros' attitude while working and how much they earned. A jornalero was required to carry the libreta when he was not working. Then it could be checked by a local official. If the work noted in the libreta did not seem to be sufficient, the jornalero could be taken to jail.

The hacendados treated the jornaleros almost like slaves. They were not paid on a regular basis. Their libretas were withheld by the hacienda owners. This prevented the jornaleros from leaving the haciendas. In addition, the jornaleros were required to buy food at stores owned by the hacendados. Often they ran up large debts because they were overcharged by the hacienda owners. Meanwhile, the jornaleros' wages were low. As a result, they could only afford to buy meager amounts of food. The jornaleros were so poor that they had to live in run-down, wooden huts.

The Spanish Government and the Poor

By the middle of the nineteenth century, the economy of Puerto Rico was controlled by a relatively small number of wealthy colonists. Most people were poor. The official poverty rate was about 70 percent.[15] There were few schools on the island. Towns had little money to construct school buildings or hire teachers. As a result, few people could read. The illiteracy rate was about 85 percent in the 1860s.[16]

Political freedom in the colony had briefly flourished in the early part of the century. But it had disappeared. After losing their other colonies in Latin America, the Spanish government had tightened its control over Puerto Rico. The cabildos had lost most of their power in local government. Spanish officials attended their meetings. These officials made sure the cabildos received the approval of

Many poor people worked on large estates, or haciendas. This painting depicts a hacienda in Ponce.

the Spanish government for all of their decisions. Meanwhile taxes on the towns grew heavier. Puerto Ricans were required to contribute to the support of Spanish troops in other parts of Spain's empire. In addition, islanders had to pay taxes to support their towns. They also had to support the Puerto Rican colonial government and the Catholic Church.

During the 1850s, Governor Juan de la Pezuela issued new laws. These laws restricted the freedom of the Creoles. According to one historian:

> By the mid-1860s the inhabitants of the colony were forbidden to hold meetings, dances, and social

> gatherings unless these had been approved by the government. Anyone who dared to challenge the system was arrested, fined, and perhaps even jailed. No one could move about after curfew (generally set at 9 p.m.), change residence, read prohibited books, or publish anything the government considered offensive.[17]

Governors shut down newspapers and exiled their publishers. Ramón Betances, a Creole doctor, tried to form an abolitionist society. The abolitionists wanted to free the slaves. But Betances was forced by the government to flee the country.

Over the next decades, however, the abolitionist movement would grow in Puerto Rico. In addition, the colonists, led by Betances and other Creoles, would succeed in forcing the Spanish government to reform the government. This would bring new freedoms to Puerto Rico.

Chapter 5

The Spanish-American War

Many Puerto Ricans felt oppressed by Spanish rule. But it took a few men, dedicated to change, to actually plan a revolution. Among them was Ramón Betances, a Puerto Rican, who had been exiled by the Spanish for his revolutionary activities and had left the island to live in Santo Domingo. Once out of Puerto Rico, Betances continued his efforts to throw off Spanish rule from the island of Santo Domingo. In 1868, his plans turned into action in a brief revolt, known as El Grito de Lares. Successful at first, the revolt was rapidly put down by the Spanish authorities in Puerto Rico. Nevertheless, it foretold what would occur only a few decades later.

The Leaders of Change

While El Grito de Lares was being planned, the Spanish queen Isabel II was being overthrown. The new government was far more liberal than the Spanish monarchy. Liberal politicians in Spain recognized it was time for a change. They realized that it was in their best interests to grant more freedom to the colonists in Puerto Rico. On the nearby island of Cuba, the Spanish colonial government was battling a revolution aimed at independence. The Spanish feared that Cuban revolutionaries might join with Puerto Ricans. Together, they might launch a new revolt in Puerto Rico.

In 1868, the Spanish government invited Puerto Ricans to send representatives to the Cortes. These representatives presented their proposals for changing the political situation in Puerto Rico. They asked for the abolition of slavery. They also wanted the same rights as Spanish citizens to vote in local elections and run the government. A powerful Spanish governor in Puerto Rico was opposed to many of these changes. Governor José Laureano Sanz represented the interests of the island's peninsulares, Spanish immigrants. He prohibited any discussion of abolition. He restricted voting to the peninsulares. Governor Sanz also disbanded the island's militia and replaced it with a Civil Guard made up of peninsulares. In addition, the governor set up a large spy network to report on the activities of the Creoles.

When complaints about Governor Sanz reached Spain, he was replaced. New governors during the 1870s tried to carry out some of the liberal programs of the Spanish Cortes. Gabriel Baldrich set up the Provincial Deputation. This was an elected committee that worked with the governor. In 1870, the colonists were permitted for the first time to form political parties. Many Creoles joined the Liberal Reform Party. Peninsulares formed the Conservative Party.

The next governor, Rafael Primo de Rivera, brought an end to the libreta system in Puerto Rico. In 1873, Governor Rivera permitted the political parties to

A Leader of Change in Puerto Rico

Born in Puerto Rico in 1823, Román Baldorioty de Castro went to elementary school in San Juan. Later he went to Madrid for his college education. After returning to the island, he became a teacher in San Juan.

During the 1870s, Baldorioty de Castro represented Puerto Rico at the Cortes. He was a strong advocate for the abolition of slavery and for Puerto Rican autonomy. In fact, he was called "The Father of Puerto Rican Autonomy." In 1873, he came back to Ponce, Puerto Rico. There he served as editor of the newspaper *El Derecho*. But he became so frustrated with political developments on the island that he left for the Dominican Republic.

Returning to Puerto Rico several years later, Baldorioty de Castro started the newspaper *La Cronica*. During the 1880s, he helped begin the Autonomist Party in Puerto Rico. The autocratic government in Puerto Rico ordered Baldorioty de Castro's arrest and imprisonment. While in prison, he became very ill and died in 1889.

nominate candidates who ran for elections to the cabildos. Meanwhile, the abolition of slavery began. Over the next few years, Puerto Rican slaves, over thirty-two thousand in number, were gradually freed.

The liberal trend came to an end in 1874. The Spanish republic ended, and the monarchy returned. That same year, Governor Sanz was sent back to Puerto Rico. He refused to work with the Provincial Deputation. Governor Sanz also prevented the Creoles from voting in local elections. Sanz was followed by several other Spanish governors who ruled as virtual dictators in Puerto Rico.

Nevertheless, the leaders of the Liberal Reform Party continued to meet. Their meetings were aimed at changing the political situation on the island. Among the leaders of the party was Román Baldorioty de Castro. He championed the idea of Puerto Rican autonomy. This meant that the island would have its own government, including an elected legislature. The Puerto Rican government could then run its own affairs within the Spanish empire.

Achieving More Rights

During the 1880s, the Liberal Reform Party was renamed the Autonomist Party of Puerto Rico (PAP). In 1887, the PAP launched a campaign against the peninsulares in local elections. During the campaign, violence broke out against the PAP candidates. In retaliation, the PAP boycotted—refused to do business with—the stores owned by peninsulares. The peninsulares asked the governor, Romualdo Palacio, to clamp down on the PAP. Many of the PAP leaders, including Román Baldorioty de Castro, were rounded up and thrown into prison. This was called "The Terrible Year of 1887."[1]

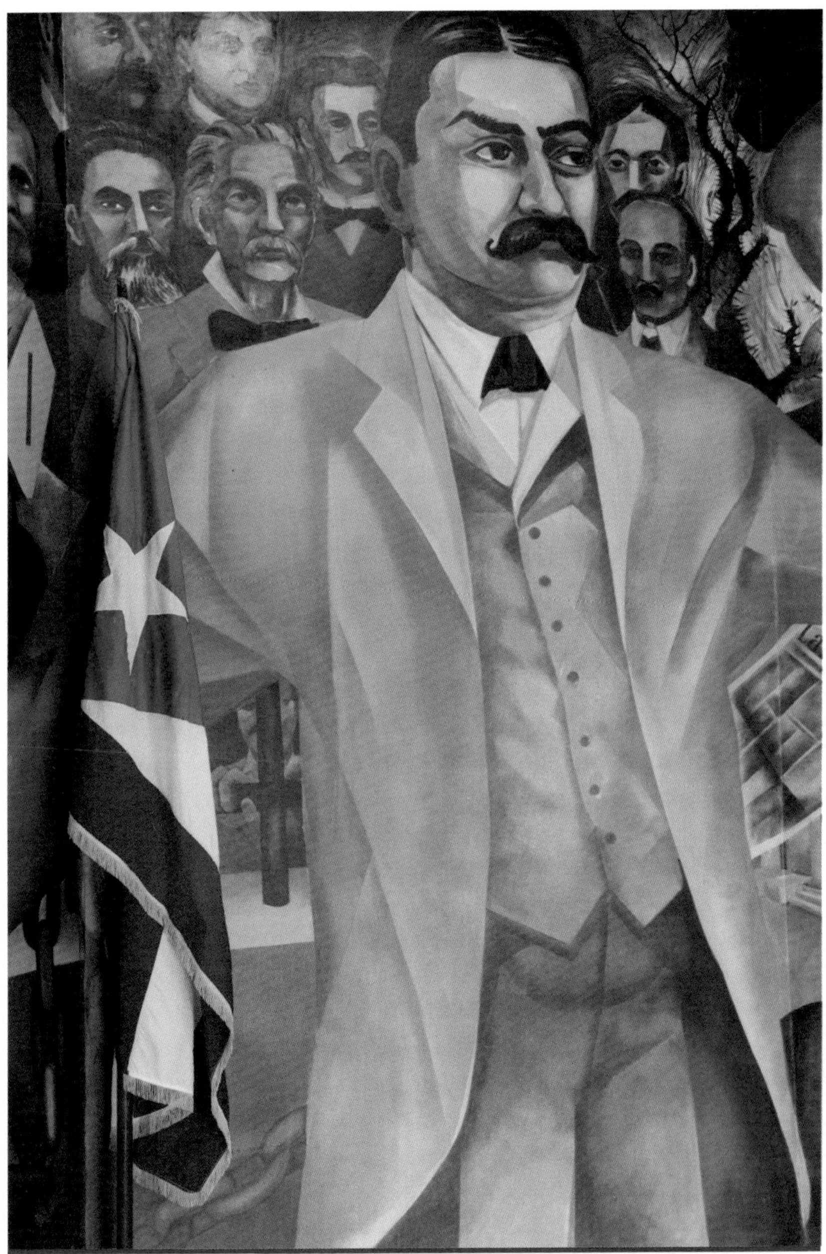

Governor Rafael Primo de Rivera ended the libreta system in Puerto Rico.

The PAP complained to the Spanish government. Palacio was replaced with a new governor. Meanwhile, a debate had broken out in the Autonomist Party. Some members wanted to end the boycott against the peninsulares. Another group, led by Luis Muñoz Rivera, wanted to hold out against the peninsulares and push for autonomy. Muñoz Rivera favored an alliance with any party in Spain that supported the viewpoint of the Autonomist Party. It took almost a decade for the alliance to develop. Finally a Spanish political party that favored autonomy came to power in Spain. It was led by Prime Minister Praxedes Mateo Sagasta. In 1897, he agreed to grant autonomy to Puerto Rico.

The situation in Cuba had convinced Spain to act. The Cuban rebels had been carrying on a war of liberation for many years. Spanish military leaders had used brutal methods to try to end the rebellion. Meanwhile, in the United States, the American press was printing stories about the brutality of the Spanish-controlled Cuban government.

The Republican administration of US President William McKinley sent a strong message to the Spanish government. The note called on the Spanish to change their policies and bring peace to Cuba. McKinley wanted the Spanish to assure the United States "that early and certain peace can be promptly secured; and that otherwise the United States must consider itself free to take steps as its Government should deem necessary to procure the result, with due regard to its own interests and the general tranquility."[2] The Spanish government feared that the United States might invade Cuba. Therefore, Spain announced that it would give Cuba and Puerto Rico autonomy.

Under the Autonomic Charter, Puerto Rico designed a new government. The government included a Puerto Rican parliament with two chambers. The House of Representatives was elected by the votes of the colonists. All males in Puerto Rico were given the right to vote. The Council of Administration was partially elected and partially appointed by the Spanish governor. The new parliament had responsibility for local affairs. These included education, finances, public health, and road building. The governor still commanded the army and controlled foreign affairs.

In March 1898, elections were held for the new parliament. Muñoz Rivera and his party won a large majority of seats. This meant that Muñoz Rivera would lead the cabinet that advised the Spanish governor. But just before the new parliament was about to open, the United States and Spain went to war. A short time afterward, the United States invaded Puerto Rico.

1898: War Breaks Out

The invasion of Puerto Rico was part of the Spanish-American War. Since the early nineteenth century, the United States had taken a major interest in the Caribbean. In 1823, the Spanish colonies were becoming independent. US President James Monroe issued the Monroe Doctrine, stating that the United States opposed any attempt by European countries to establish new colonies in the Western Hemisphere. Nevertheless, President Monroe added "with the existing colonies or dependencies of any European power we have not interfered and shall not interfere."[3] These colonies included Cuba and Puerto Rico. They remained part of the Spanish empire. In the 1840s, President James Polk offered to purchase Cuba. But the

Spanish government did not sell the island to the United States.

During the last part of the nineteenth century, the United States began building up its navy. American ships sailed along the Atlantic seaboard and in the Pacific Ocean. These ships were powered by coal. Therefore, the United States began to acquire coaling stations on islands in the Pacific Ocean. American ships could be docked at these islands to refuel. In addition, American political leaders recognized that they needed a way for warships to travel quickly from the Atlantic to the Pacific. Therefore, officials began to plan to build a canal across the Isthmus of Panama. This was a short strip of land located in Latin America. To protect the entrance to the canal, US leaders thought about acquiring islands in the Caribbean. In 1890, US Secretary of State James G. Blaine wrote, "I think there are only three places that are of value enough to be taken; one is Hawaii and the others are Cuba and Puerto Rico."[4]

In 1897, the United States annexed—took control of—the independent island of Hawaii. The island had rich sugar plantations that were owned by American investors. The annexation of Hawaii provided protection for the American west coast. In addition, Hawaii gave the United States an important position in the Pacific Ocean. For many years the United States had traded with China. Some American politicians feared that this trade might be jeopardized by Spain. The Spanish controlled the Philippine Islands off the coast of Asia.

As the rebellion in Cuba continued, some Americans favored an invasion by the United States. Among them was Senator Henry Cabot Lodge, a powerful Republican leader. Another advocate of war was Theodore Roosevelt, who was then assistant secretary of the Navy. As Roosevelt wrote, "It is very difficult for me not to wish for a war with Spain, for such a war would result at once in getting us a proper navy and a good system of coast defense."[5]

In February, the American battleship USS *Maine* exploded in the harbor of Havana, Cuba. The ship had been sent to Havana to protect Americans living in Cuba. No one was sure of the cause of the explosion. But newspapers in the United States accused the Spanish of blowing up the ship. The disaster took the lives of over two hundred sixty American sailors. Two months later, the United States declared war on Spain.

The USS *Maine* exploded on February 15, 1898, in the Havana Harbor, Cuba. Here lifeboats can be seen rescuing the crew from the battleship.

After war began, American forces moved swiftly. In the Pacific, a naval squadron under the command of Commodore George Dewey steamed toward Manila, capital of the Philippines. After a brief battle on May 1, Dewey destroyed the Spanish fleet guarding the capital. Meanwhile, American troops gathered in Florida for an invasion of Cuba. Among them was Theodore Roosevelt. He was leading a cavalry squadron known as the Rough Riders.

The American forces sailed for Cuba, landing near Santiago in June. The US infantry won a battle against the Spanish defenders on San Juan Heights outside Santiago. Then the American army laid siege to the city. Santiago fell on July 16, 1898.

Next, US forces turned their attention to Puerto Rico. The island had been opened to free trade during the nineteenth century. As a result, it had become a major market for US goods. In addition, Puerto Rico had strategic importance. One of the major supporters of American naval power was Captain Alfred Thayer Mahan. In his books, Mahan pointed out that powerful nations had strong navies. Mahan's writings influenced many political leaders in the United States, including Theodore Roosevelt. Mahan regarded Puerto Rico as an important part of the US "defense network." He emphasized that no European power could gain control of the Caribbean "with a United States fleet based upon Puerto Rico and the adjacent islands."[6]

Puerto Rican exiles lived in New York City. They strongly supported independence for the island. They had joined with Cuban revolutionary leaders who had set up an organization in New York. Together, they called for the

Shortly after the start of the Spanish-American War, US warships attacked Spanish forces in San Juan, Puerto Rico.

General Nelson Miles led the American invasion of Puerto Rico in 1898.

independence of both islands. José Julio Henna was the leader of the Puerto Rican independence group in New York. He was a friend of Senator Henry Cabot Lodge and Secretary Roosevelt. After the war began over Cuba, Roosevelt told Lodge that the conflict should continue "until we get Puerto Rico." Lodge agreed with this strategy.[7]

US forces invaded Puerto Rico on July 25, 1898. They were under the command of General Nelson Miles. Miles's troops landed at Guánica, which was only lightly defended by the Spanish. Next, the American fleet headed to Ponce on July 27. There was little resistance from the Puerto Ricans as American troops marched into the city. At Ponce, Miles issued a proclamation:

> We have not come to make war upon the people of a country that for centuries has been oppressed, but, on the contrary, to bring you protection, not only to yourselves but to your property, to promote your prosperity, and to bestow upon you the . . . blessings of the liberal institutions of our government.[8]

Yet at the same time, Miles told his own military officers that "the power of the military occupant [must be] absolute and supreme. . . ."[9]

With about thirty-five hundred soldiers, Miles continued inland from Ponce. He took control of other towns. The American forces were assisted by Creoles, who drove out the Spanish town officials. Miles received reinforcements of about eight thousand troops in early August. Soon he controlled much of the island.

Many Puerto Ricans hoped that the invasion would benefit the island. They expected that Puerto Rico might become independent or at least be given autonomy by the

United States.[10] A peace agreement between Spain and the United States was reached on August 12, 1898. The Spanish agreed to leave Puerto Rico. Until that time, the Autonomist government of Muñoz Rivera remained in power in San Juan, which had not been occupied by US forces. In other parts of the island, violence erupted. Pardidas, groups of armed men, began to attack stores owned by peninsulares. Attacks occurred in Mayagüez, Anasco, and other communities. On October 18, 1898, the last Spanish soldiers left Puerto Rico. President McKinley established a military government to run the island. Once again, the island's desire for autonomy or independence would be denied.

Chapter 6

Puerto Rico Changes Direction

Puerto Ricans expected that the Spanish-American War, by ending Spain's rule of the island, would bring the same type of democratic government that the United States enjoyed. Indeed, General Miles had said that he and his men "come bearing the banner of freedom."[1] But the reverse happened under American rule.

During the first two years of United States control, from 1898 to 1900, the island was run by several military governors. They believed that Puerto Rico was not ready for self-government. Therefore, they ended the autonomy that the island had received just before the start of the Spanish-American War. One of these governors was General Guy Henry. He wrote that his job was "giving them [the Puerto Ricans] Kindergarten instruction in controlling themselves without allowing them too much liberty."[2] Another governor, General George W. Davis, wrote about "the general unfitness of the great mass of the people for self-government. . . ."[3] The early governors immediately dismantled the Puerto Rican government.

The legislature was disbanded in 1898. The following year, the cabinet was also eliminated. The military governor ran the country without the Puerto Rican political leaders.

One of the primary concerns of General Henry was the education of the Puerto Rican people. His aim was to teach the people patriotism. That is, he wanted them to pledge allegiance to the United States. Students were also required to learn how to speak English. In fact, according to historian Pedro A. Caban, "He ordered that all of Puerto Rico's teachers learn to speak English and instructed the municipal [town] authorities to hire only teachers fluent in English."[4] Over the next ten years, the number of elementary schools was almost doubled. Illiteracy on the island in English and Spanish declined from almost 80 percent to 66 percent.[5]

In 1900, the military governors were replaced by a civilian governor. The first civilian governor was Charles Herbert Allen. He had served as assistant secretary of the Navy. Allen ran the country under the guidelines set up by the Foraker Act. This law had been passed by Congress in 1900. According to the Foraker Act, the governor was appointed by the president of the United States. He governed with the help of an Executive Council that included six Americans and five Puerto Ricans. The act provided for a legislative assembly elected by Puerto Ricans. But only those who could read and write, and who paid taxes, could vote. The governor could veto any act passed by the legislature. He also had the power to appoint members to the local cabildos.

Some Puerto Ricans supported the new government. The local Republican Party, largely made up of peninsulares, "applauded the Foraker Act."[6] In part, this was because party members received political jobs by supporting the American government in Puerto Rico.

The Federal Party, led by Luis Muñoz Rivera, opposed the new government. Muñoz Rivera left the island and moved to New York. His party also refused to participate in elections in 1900. As Muñoz Rivera wrote, "In 1901, only a few of us distrusted the United States. Today [1902] all are beginning to realize that we have been deceived."[7] He criticized the legislature. It was a body that "performs useless work. . . . its initiative crashing against the perpetual wall of an Executive Council composed of six Continental Americans and five Americanized Puerto Ricans appointed by the President of the United States."[8]

Muñoz Rivera eventually returned to Puerto Rico in 1904. He formed a new political party, the Union Party. In elections that year, the Union Party took control of the legislature. The party supported self-government. Puerto Ricans who voted for the party had become thoroughly unhappy with American rule.

Economic Changes

During the early years of the American government, the economy of Puerto Rico changed. With the defeat of the Spanish, Puerto Rico was no longer part of Spain's empire. The island's products, especially coffee, had once been shipped to Spain. Very low taxes were charged by the Spanish government. Therefore, Spain and other parts of Europe became large markets for Puerto Rican coffee.

After 1898, Spain began placing heavy taxes on Puerto Rican coffee. The price of Puerto Rican coffee in Europe rose, and the market for it declined greatly. In addition, Puerto Rico was struck by a devastating hurricane in 1899. This storm destroyed over three quarters of the coffee crop.[9] Meanwhile, coffee growers were forced to pay higher taxes on their land by the new American government. As a result, many coffee growers were forced to sell their property. Much of it was bought by American companies.

At the same time, the administration of President William McKinley was encouraging American firms to invest in Puerto Rico. The island had a climate that was excellent for growing sugar. Since Puerto Rico was now part of the United States, sugar could enter the United States without any import taxes. Four American companies gradually began buying land to create large sugarcane operations. These included Central Aguirre, South Porto Rico, Fajardo, and United States Porto Rico/Eastern Sugar. By the 1920s, these companies produced over half of all the sugar exported from Puerto Rico.[10] Under the terms of the Foraker Act, no company was permitted to own more than five hundred acres of property. But the governors of the island permitted this provision of the act to be ignored. Therefore, the four large sugar companies owned large amounts of land.

American companies built large mills, called centrals. These were used for grinding up the sugarcane. The largest central, according to historian César Ayala, was Central Guánica. It was owned by the South Porto Rico Sugar Company.[11] This company, along with the other three American corporations, made arrangements with local sugar plantation owners, called colonos. The colonos brought their cane to the centrals. Each central cost a large amount of money to build. But this money was loaned to the sugar companies by US banks. They had established branches on the island. Banks also loaned American companies money to build roads and railroads. These were

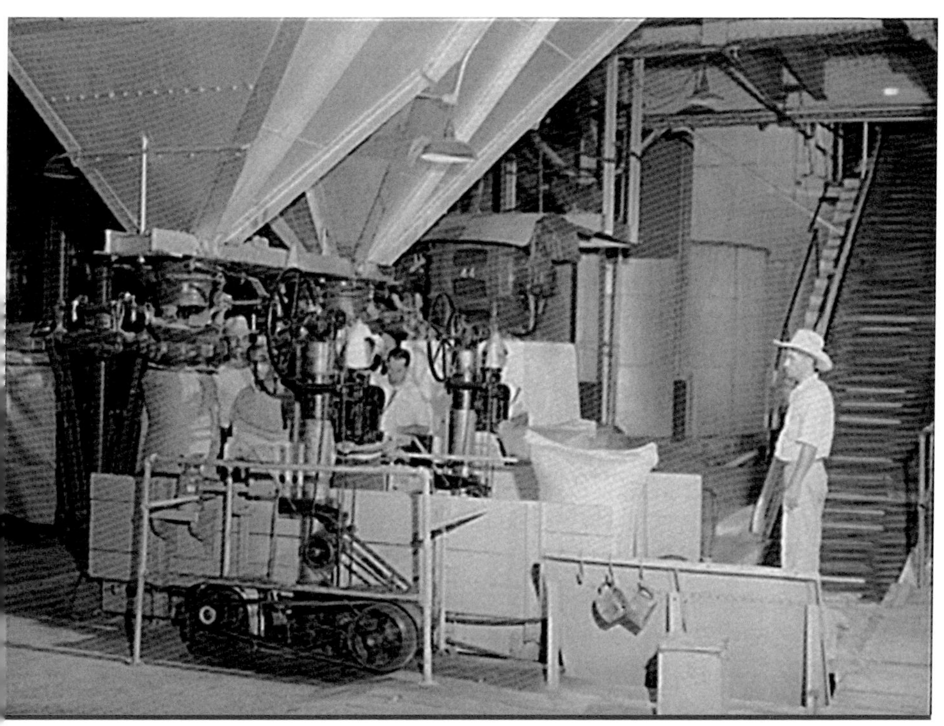

Workers weigh and sew bags of sugar at the South Puerto Rico Sugar Company.

necessary to transport the sugar to ports along the coast. From the coast, it was shipped to the United States.

Labor on the island was plentiful. Many coffee growers had lost their farms and needed work. They found jobs building roads and railroads and working in the sugarcane fields. Wages on the island were comparatively low. In 1917, a sugarcane worker made only sixty-three cents per day. By contrast, a worker earned twice this amount in Cuba.[12]

American companies also made an impact on the Puerto Rican tobacco business. Tobacco grown on the island was used for cigars. American manufacturing firms, like Porto Rican-American Tobacco Company, manufactured almost 85 percent of the cigars made from island tobacco.[13]

Puerto Rico's Political and Economic Growth

Muñoz Rivera recognized the power exercised by the United States in Puerto Rico. He believed that Puerto Rico must become an independent nation. But, according to author José Trias Monge, Muñoz Rivera "was also convinced that the United States would not grant independence to Puerto Rico in his lifetime." So he focused on trying "to obtain more self-government for his people."[14]

In 1910, Muñoz Rivera was elected resident commissioner from Puerto Rico to the United States. Under the Foraker Act, the commissioner represented the interests of the Puerto Rican people to the US Congress. As he told the congressmen, "Puerto Ricans will feel humiliated until you have abolished in the island a colonial system under which the government is not founded upon the will of the governed."[15] Muñoz Rivera lobbied hard for an improvement in the Foraker Act. Finally, in 1917, Congress passed the Jones Act. The new act gave the island a two-house legislature elected by the Puerto Rican people. In addition, Puerto Ricans became citizens of the United States. Nevertheless, the governor was still appointed by the president of the United States. Governors retained a veto over every piece of legislation passed by the legislature.

Muñoz Rivera died a year before the Jones Act was passed. However, he did get to review the legislation and was not satisfied with it. But it was the best that he could achieve.[16] During the 1920s, new political parties were formed with younger leaders. One of these parties, the Alianza, favored autonomy. Another party, called the Coalicion, wanted Puerto Rico to become an American state.

During the 1920s, the United States enjoyed a period of enormous prosperity. Nevertheless, economic conditions on the island remained poor for most Puerto Ricans. Workers made as little as one to two dollars per day. This was far less than workers made in the United States. To make matters worse, food prices in Puerto Rico were higher.[17] Much of the food had to be imported because so much land had been converted from food crops to growing sugarcane. As authors Bailey Diffie and Justin Diffie wrote in 1931:

> While sugar acreage was increasing almost four times, crops devoted to food were declining to about two thirds their former acreage. . . . Porto Rico has only one acre of food crops today for every 15 people, whereas only 30 years ago she had an acre for every six people.[18]

The Impact of Economic Depression

Economic conditions on the island grew even worse with the coming of the Great Depression. In October 1929, the New York Stock Exchange crashed. Many people were financially wiped out during the next twelve months. Businesses in the United States and other parts of the world went bankrupt. The demand for Puerto Rican sugar and other products declined. On the island, wages sunk to fifty or sixty cents per day. Unemployment, which was 30 percent in the 1920s, rose even higher to 36 percent in 1929. Severe hurricanes also affected farmers' harvests, throwing people out of work.[19]

When the Depression struck Puerto Rico, the island's governor was Theodore Roosevelt Jr. He was the son of former President Roosevelt. The governor criticized the colonial policies of the United States. He then made it a priority to ask President Herbert Hoover's administration for money to help the islanders who were out of work. Very little money was sent to Puerto Rico. Still, Roosevelt raised some funds from private donations to help the unemployed.

The Depression fueled discontent among many Puerto Ricans with the American government on the island. In 1932, a new political party was founded by Luis Muñoz Marin. He was the son of Muñoz Rivera. This party, the Puerto Rican Liberal Party, called for independence from the United States. But Muñoz Marin was less interested in independence than economics. He wanted to help the poor and unemployed improve their lives.

In 1932, Franklin D. Roosevelt was elected president of the United States. After taking office, Roosevelt began a program called the New Deal. The New Deal was an effort

A Great Puerto Rican Leader

Luis Muñoz Marin was born in Puerto Rico in 1898. But much of his childhood was spent in the United States. His father lived there during the early part of the twentieth century. Muñoz Marin was educated in the United States. As a result, he was bilingual, speaking English and Spanish. He later became a writer for *The Nation* magazine and a poet.

Like his father, Muñoz Marin also entered politics. He supported the Alianza Party. Later he broke with Alianza and formed the Liberal Party in 1932. Muñoz Marin was a very effective public speaker. During the late 1930s, Muñoz Marin broke with the Liberal Party and formed a new political group. It was called the Popular Democratic Party (PDP), founded in 1938.

During the 1940s, he worked closely with the American governor in Puerto Rico, Rexford Tugwell. Together they helped revive the Puerto Rican economy. Muñoz Marin became the first elected Puerto Rican governor of the island in 1949. He was reelected several times, serving through 1964. Then he became a senator in the Puerto Rican legislature. Muñoz Marin died in 1980.

Theodore Roosevelt Jr. was governor of Puerto Rico from 1929 to 1932. As governor, he encouraged the United States to help unemployed Puerto Ricans.

to help the unemployed in the United States return to work. Some money from the New Deal was also funneled into Puerto Rico. This money was administered by the Puerto Rico Reconstruction Administration (PRRA). Between 1935 and 1938, about $58 million was spent on the island by the Roosevelt administration.[20] The money was used for construction projects like new manufacturing plants. These projects employed out-of-work Puerto Ricans.

Nevertheless, discontent remained high on the island. Strikes had broken out during the 1930s among the sugarcane workers. They were protesting low wages. The Nationalist Party, led by Pedro Albizu Campos, called on Puerto Ricans to begin a revolution. Albizu Campos wanted the island to achieve independence. Mass demonstrations and violence broke out in 1935. Police tried to arrest several members of the Nationalist Party. Four of them and one policeman died in a gun battle.

Early in 1936, Nationalists assassinated Francis Riggs. He was the American in charge of the island's police force. When two Nationalists were arrested for the assassination, they were murdered by police. Albizu Campos was later arrested and charged with trying to overthrow the government. Albizu Campos was found guilty and sent to prison. The following year, violence broke out at a Nationalist parade in Ponce. After a shot was fired, police at the parade site opened fire. Nineteen Puerto Ricans died, and many more were wounded. The Ponce Massacre, as it was called, brought an end to the violent demonstrations. But discontent on the island continued.

How Operation Bootstrap and Other Programs Changed the Island

By 1940, unemployment on the island was still high. That year Muñoz Marin and the Popular Democratic Party (PDP) ran on a platform of improving the Puerto Rican economy. The party campaigned on a simple theme: "Bread, Land, and Liberty."[21] After winning the election, Muñoz Marin became the leader of the Puerto Rican legislature. In this position, he worked closely with the new governor of Puerto Rico, Rexford Tugwell.

Appointed late in 1941, Tugwell had been a member of the Roosevelt administration. He was committed to improving living conditions for the poor on the island. Meanwhile, Puerto Rico had become a key island in the defense of the Caribbean. In 1939, Germany began World War II. German submarines entered the Caribbean and threatened Latin America. Shortly after Tugwell became governor, the United States was attacked by Japanese forces at Pearl Harbor, Hawaii. The United States entered the war against Japan and its ally Germany. American leaders realized that large-scale dissatisfaction in Puerto Rico might impact the war effort. It would be much harder to defend the Panama Canal against a possible attack by Germany.

During the 1940s, Tugwell and Muñoz Marin worked together to improve the Puerto Rican economy. Among the new economic programs they began was the Development Bank of Puerto Rico. This government-run bank made loans to small businesses, especially in construction. Another economic program was the Puerto Rico Development Company. The company funded several new businesses. Among them was the Puerto Rico Glass

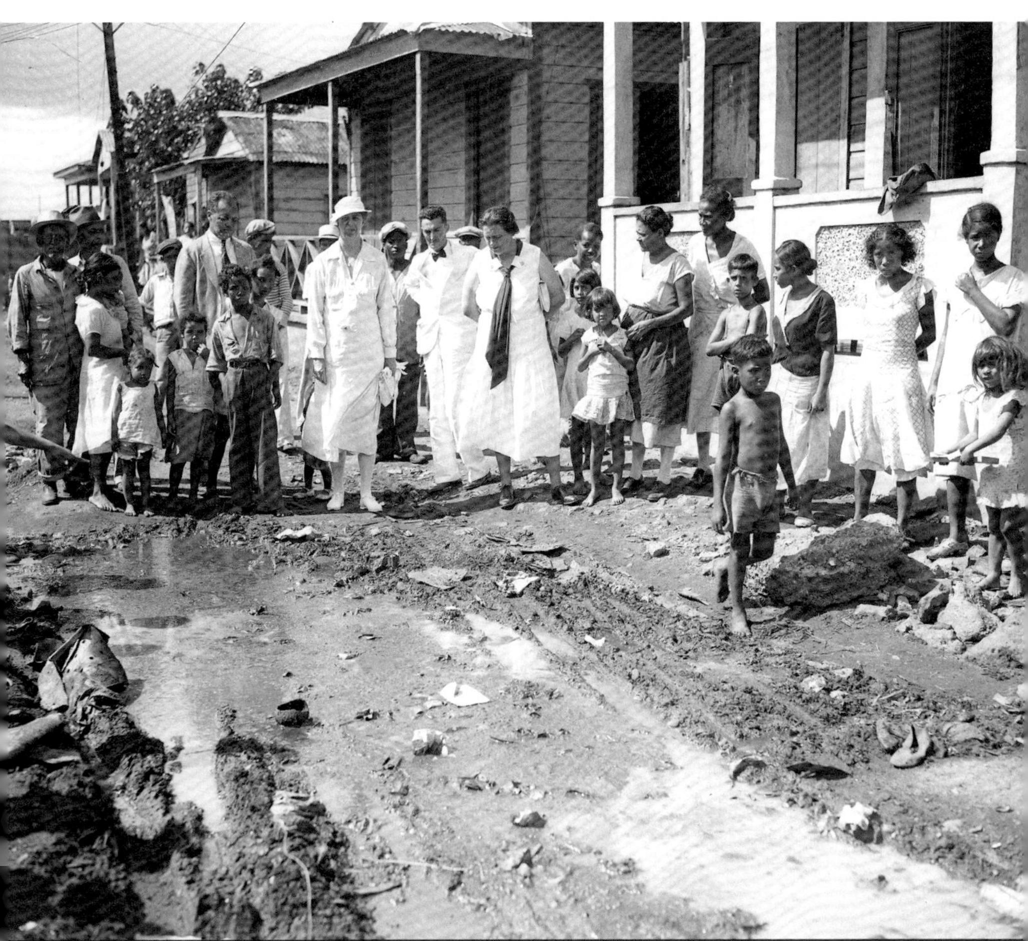

Eleanor Roosevelt, wife of President Franklin D. Roosevelt, visits a neighborhood in San Juan. She was very moved by the poverty and poor conditions that she saw there and vowed to do what she could to help.

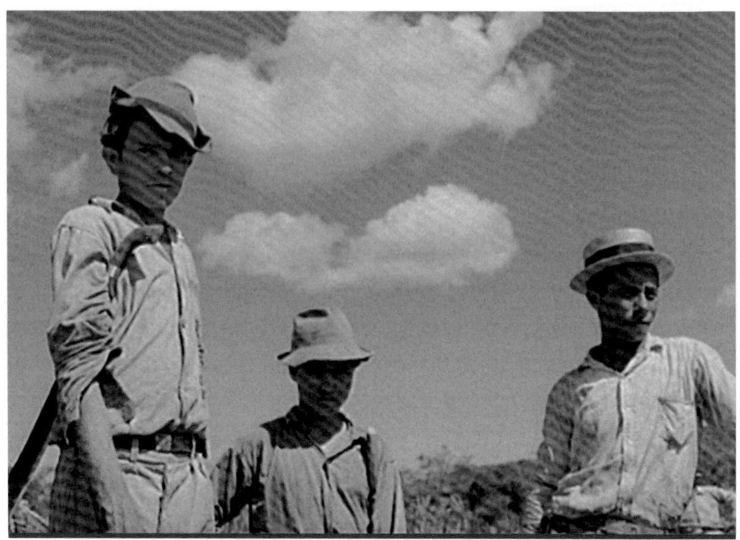

These paid workers take a break from harvesting sugarcane in 1941. In the eighteenth century, the Spanish had often used African slaves to avoid paying farm workers.

Company. It manufactured bottles for rum, which was made from sugarcane. Another company manufactured paper cartons for rum and other products. And the Puerto Rico Clay Product Corporation made bricks used in the construction business.

In addition to setting up new companies, the governor and the PDP made changes in land ownership. They enforced the provision in the Jones Act that limited companies to owning five hundred acres of land. American corporations were required to sell large land holdings to the government. These in turn were managed by small Puerto Rican farmers who shared in the profits.

During the 1940s, the island also tried to attract manufacturing concerns to the island. This was an effort to change the economy from its heavy emphasis on agriculture. US firms were offered low rents for buildings. They were also required to pay low corporate income taxes. This new program was called Operation Bootstrap. It helped transform the island's economy during the 1950s.

While the economy of the island was changing, there were also new political developments. In 1943, President Roosevelt proposed that the island of Puerto Rico should elect its own governor. This legislation was extremely important to Muñoz Marin. Roosevelt died in 1945 before the new legislation was passed. In 1946, President Harry Truman appointed the first Puerto Rican governor, Jesus Piñero. Piñero had been the Puerto Rican resident commissioner in Washington. In 1947, the bill was signed by President Truman for Puerto Ricans to elect their governor. The following year Muñoz Marin and his political party won the election. He became the first elected Puerto Rican governor of the island.

Luis Muñoz Marin sought to improve the economy of Puerto Rico by supporting small businesses and bringing American companies to the island.

Self-Government for Puerto Rico

Luis Muñoz Marin focused on two issues after he was elected governor: a different relationship with the United States and an improvement in the island's economy. For more than six decades, these issues were central to Puerto Rico's future.

Self-Government

In 1948, when he ran for election as governor, Muñoz Marin told the Puerto Rican people that the system of government had to change. As he said, "all of us, absolutely all of us, wish that this obsolete system, which we call a colonial system is ended. The form of political relationship in which the United States holds Puerto Rico is not just."[1] Under the colonial system, laws passed by the governor and congress of Puerto Rico needed the approval of the US government. Muñoz Marin traveled to Washington, DC, to present his views about changing this system.

Muñoz Marin appeared before Congress in 1949. He was asked by Representative William Lemke, "May I sum it up this way: You prefer self government under the

Federal Government of the United States?" Muñoz Marin replied, "That is right. . . ."[2] Muñoz had in mind a form of government known as a commonwealth. In his mind, this meant that Puerto Rico would no longer be a possession or colony of the United States. Laws in Puerto Rico would not be changed without the consent of both the Puerto Rican and the United States governments.[3]

This was Governor Muñoz Marin's view. But it was not the view of the United States. In 1950, the Congress passed Public Law 600. This law gave Puerto Ricans the right to create their own constitution to govern the island. However, Public Law 600 emphasized that the island still "belonged" to the United States. The island was a US colony.[4]

Some Puerto Ricans were strongly opposed to Public Law 600. Among them were members of the Puerto Rican Nationalist Party. This party supported independence. It was still led by Pedro Albizu Campos, who had been released from prison in 1947. In the fall of 1950, groups of armed Nationalists staged revolts in towns across the island. A small group of Nationalists also tried to assassinate Governor Muñoz Marin. But they were unsuccessful. On November 1, 1950, two Nationalists, Oscar Collazo and Griselio Torresola, made an assassination attempt on President Truman. Collazo was wounded and Torresola was killed by guards protecting the president's house.

In the midst of the violence, Puerto Ricans voted in 1951 to write a new constitution. The constitutional convention was led by the PDP, Governor Muñoz Marin's party. These delegates created the Commonwealth of Puerto Rico. Under the commonwealth, the island had its own governor, congress, and court system. But Puerto Ricans

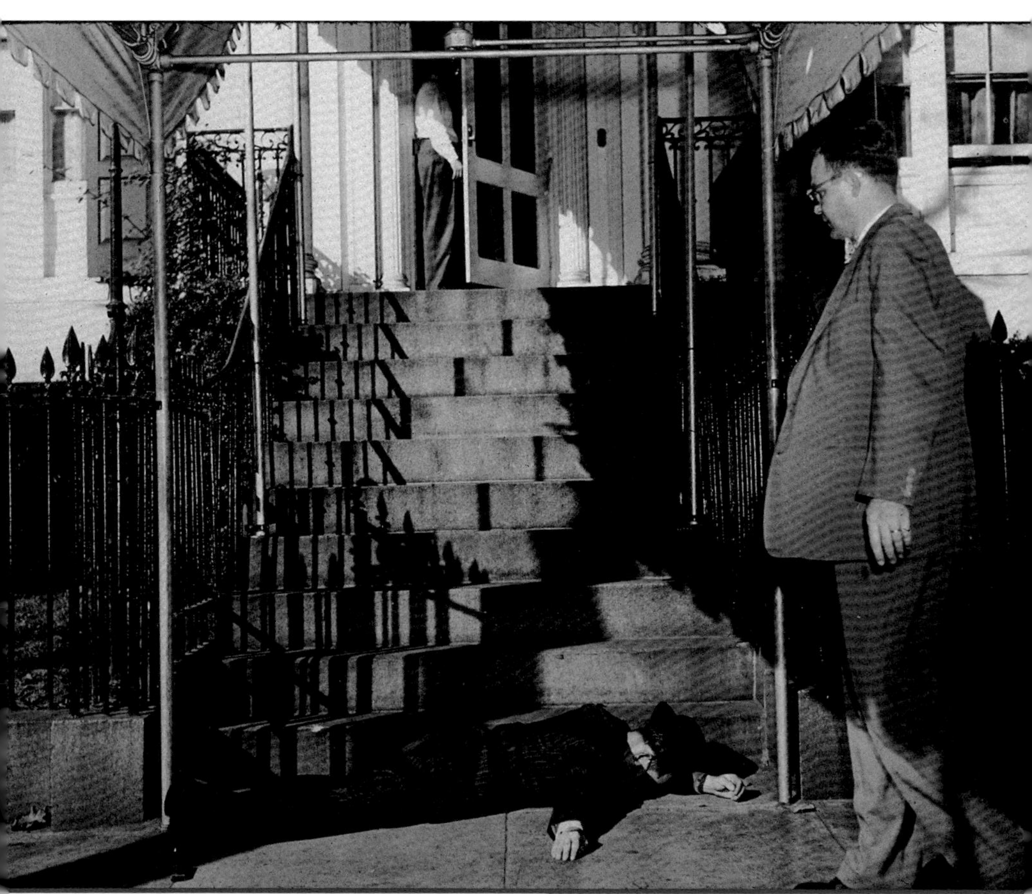

Puerto Rican Nationalists Oscar Collazo and Griselio Torresola tried to assassinate President Harry S. Truman on November 1, 1950. Here, Collazo lies wounded after the failed attempt.

still could not vote in American presidential elections. Nor did they have the ability to elect congressmen and senators to represent Puerto Rico in the US Congress. The island still had a resident commissioner who represented its interests in Washington, DC. But the commissioner had no vote in Congress. The new constitution was approved by the US Congress in 1952.

As José Trias Monge wrote:

> Puerto Rico was not being groomed . . . for independence or statehood. Puerto Rico was to be held . . . as long as needed, firmly under the control of Congress, as a useful guardian of eastern access to the Panama Canal, a key part of the security system for the Caribbean area. . . .[5]

As historian James Dietz added, "The island remained a colony, though now the United States could and did claim that the association of Puerto Rico with the United States was voluntary and had been approved by Puerto Rican voters, who had also written their own constitution."[6]

All Puerto Ricans, however, did not approve of the new constitution. In 1954, members of the Nationalist Party entered the gallery of the US House of Representatives. Once inside, they began firing shots at congressmen on the floor of the House. Five members of Congress were wounded. The three Puerto Ricans, Rafael Cancel Miranda, Lolita Lebron, and Andres Cordero, were captured. They were later tried and sent to prison.

Muñoz Marin continued serving as governor through 1964. During this period, he tried to change the commonwealth's relationship with the United States. But Congress refused to make any changes.[7]

Important Changes for the Island

After completing his fourth term as governor, Muñoz Marin stepped down. He was succeeded by Roberto Sanchez Vilella, a close associate of Muñoz Marin who won the election of 1964. Meanwhile a Status Commission had been formed. The commission included members from the United States and Puerto Rico. It continued to look into the status of Puerto Rico as a commonwealth. The commission called for Puerto Ricans to hold a plebiscite, or vote, on the island's status. They could vote for independence, statehood, or commonwealth with a relationship of equality between the United States and Puerto Rico. In 1967, an overwhelming majority voted for a new commonwealth status. But, as José Trias Monge put it, "Congress did not pay the slightest attention to the expression of the popular will in Puerto Rico. . . . "[8]

During 1968, there was a split in the PDP. Some political leaders in Puerto Rico had formed a new political group called the New Progressive Party (NPP). The leader of the party, Luis A. Ferre, was elected governor. The NPP supported statehood for Puerto Rico, which was gaining support across the island. But many people still supported the commonwealth. During the 1970s and 1980s, Puerto Ricans elected the leader of either the PDP or NPP as governor of the island.

One of the major issues confronting these governors was the island's economy. During the 1950s and 1960s, the economy had continued to grow under Operation Bootstrap. Growth was more than 8 percent annually in the fifties. It reached almost 11 percent per year in the sixties. Between 1950 and 1980, Puerto Ricans enjoyed enormous growth in personal incomes, from an average of $342 per year in

1950 to $3,479 in 1980.[9] American businesses were lured to the island because they did not have to pay corporate income taxes. In addition, wages in Puerto Rico were much lower than in the United States. In 1980, they were just over half of what American workers earned.[10]

New businesses were mainly located in the island's cities. As a result, many Puerto Ricans left the countryside to move to San Juan and other urban areas. Some worked in chemical and pharmaceutical businesses. Others were employed in machinery and metal manufacturing firms. Still others worked in the tourist industry. Hotels began to spring up on the island to lure American tourists who came south, especially in winter, to escape the cold weather in the United States.

At the same time, fewer and fewer people were working in agriculture. Much of the food eaten by Puerto Ricans was imported from the United States. As historian James Dietz pointed out, Puerto Rican leaders emphasized industry and let agriculture decline. They believed that agriculture could not provide enough jobs for the island's growing population. But as Dietz said, "the choice need not have been either agriculture *or* industry; it could have been a mix of agriculture *and* industry. . . ."[11]

Unfortunately, industry did not create enough jobs for Puerto Ricans. By the early 1980s, unemployment on the island had grown to over 23 percent of the workforce.[12] This was much higher than in the United States. To help Puerto Ricans deal with the unemployment problem, the United States offered islanders the Food Stamp Program. This program was started on the island under the administration of President Richard Nixon during the 1970s. Food stamps were freely given to the poor in the United States and in Puerto Rico. On the island, 75 percent of the population lived below the US poverty line. As a result, they began receiving stamps to purchase food in local markets.[13]

According to author Ronald Fernandez, the Food Stamp Program had a negative effect on the island's economy:

> If people worked in legitimate occupations, they showed income which made them ineligible for stamps. Thus, more and more Puerto Ricans either refused to work, or if they did so, . . .accepted cash payments "under the table" [without reporting them].[14]

In addition, any agriculture left in Puerto Rico was hurt by the Food Stamp Program. With food stamps, it was much cheaper for Puerto Ricans to buy imported food in the supermarkets, which accepted the stamps.[15] Local farmers could not afford to accept them.

The combination of food stamps and unemployment created a major problem for Puerto Rican political leaders. One way they tried to solve the problem was to expand the commonwealth government and hire more people. By the mid-1980s, almost one quarter of all Puerto Rican workers were employed by the government.[16]

Despite the government's efforts, the lack of opportunity on the island continued to have a major impact on Puerto Ricans. During the 1990s, 30 percent of high school students dropped out before graduation. There were no jobs available for many of them after graduation. The drop-out rate was almost three times the rate in the United States. In addition, Puerto Rico became a center of the illegal drug trade.[17]

Weapons Testing on Vieques

The island of Vieques off the coast of Puerto Rico was a source of conflict with the United States for many years. Beginning in the 1940s, the US Navy tested its weapons on the small island. Residents of Vieques and many other Puerto Ricans opposed the tests. The tests endangered plant and animal life as well as the lives of the residents themselves.

In 1978, fishermen led protests against the US Navy. One protestor, Angel Rodriguez Cristobal, was sent to prison in Florida, where he was murdered. In response to the murder, a Puerto Rican group named Los Macheteros killed two American sailors on a bus in 1979. Then, in 1983, Los Macheteros robbed a bank of $7.1 million in Connecticut.

In 1999, a resident of the island was killed accidentally by a navy warplane. As a result, President Bill Clinton agreed to gradually end all weapons testing. The navy finally left Vieques in 2003.

Today, many residents of Vieques claim that they have become sick from chemicals used during the years of weapons testing. A large group of people brought a lawsuit against the US government, but the case was thrown out in 2012.[18]

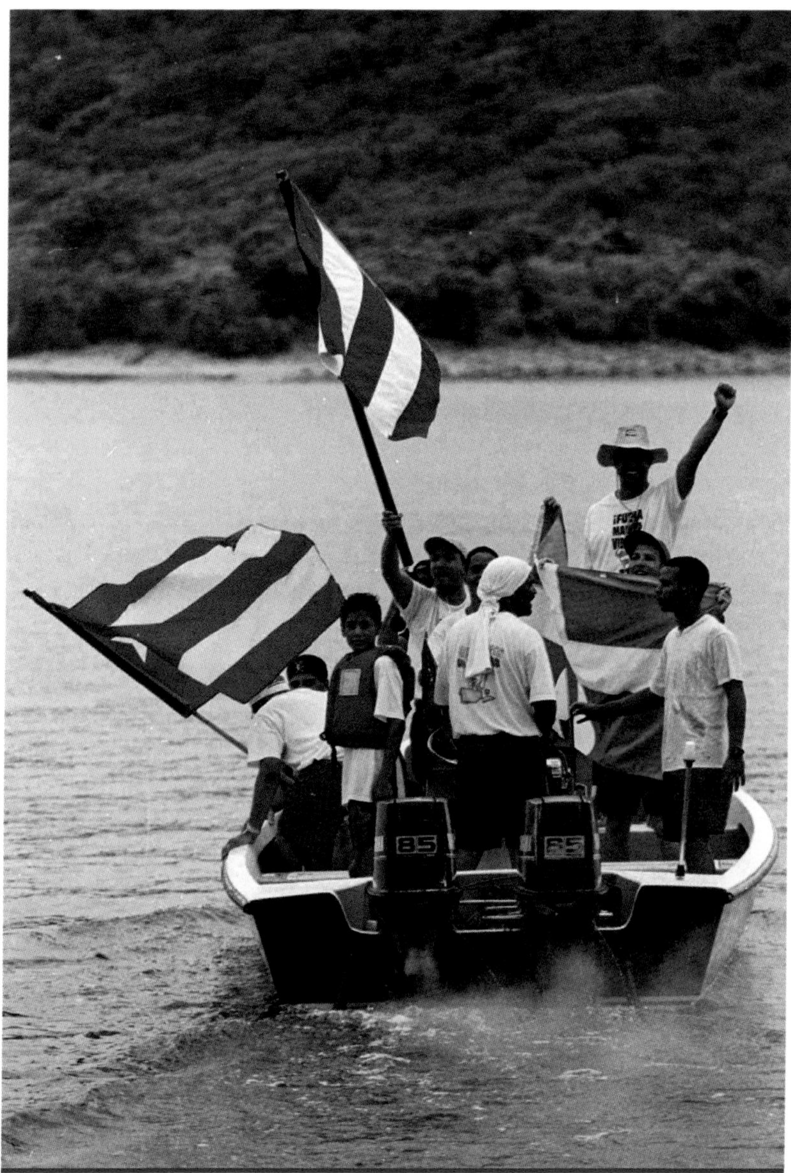

In May 2003, a group of protestors marked the end of US Navy bombing on Vieques Island.

Major Concerns of the People

During the 1990s, the status of Puerto Rico and the economy continued to be major issues on the island. In 1992, Pedro Rossello, a doctor and leader of the NPP, was elected governor of Puerto Rico. Rossello was a strong advocate of statehood for Puerto Rico. Shortly after taking office, Puerto Rican leaders approved a plan to hold another plebiscite. Puerto Ricans were asked to vote on the same options as before. This time 48 percent of voters chose the commonwealth option. About 46 percent voted for statehood, and 4 percent wanted independence.[19] Much to the disappointment of the NPP, a majority had not supported statehood.

To many Puerto Ricans, statehood had advantages as well as disadvantages. If Puerto Rico became a state, its citizens could vote in presidential elections. In addition, they could elect members to Congress. This would give them a greater say in their own future. But many Puerto Ricans also feared that becoming a state might cause them to lose their identity. As Ruben Berrios Martinez, a leader of the independence movement, wrote, "For us, 'we the people' means we Puerto Ricans. . . . As a state, Puerto Rico is bound to pay the heaviest of prices: cultural assimilation . . . which would subordinate the island's Spanish language and distinct culture."[20]

Many people on the island speak little English. As Ralph de Toledano put it, "The upper classes speak English, but the language of the island is Spanish. As a state, Puerto Rico's official language would have to be English, which would create a deep and poisonous conflict. . . . "[21] As a result, a majority of Puerto Ricans still hope to achieve an improvement in the commonwealth form of government. They oppose statehood.

The issue of status continues to be discussed in Puerto Rico and in the halls of the American Congress. In 1996, Congressman Don Young of Alaska introduced a bill for another vote on the future of the island. In 1998, islanders voted again. They could choose between statehood, independence, the commonwealth, or none of the above. Statehood had the support of 47 percent of the voters. But 50 percent voted for "none of the above." According to interviews with these voters, they said they supported no change in the government.[22]

Meanwhile, Puerto Rican political leaders continued to struggle with the island's economy. During the 1990s, tourism on the island remained strong. Over 4 million tourists visited Puerto Rico annually. This number reached five million annually by the early part of the twenty-first century. But poverty remained a serious problem. Half the island's population of 4 million was considered poor. Unemployment was at least 12 percent of the adult workforce, more than double the rate in the United States.[23]

In the governor's election of 2000, the economy was a major issue. Governor Rosello had decided not to run for reelection. His administration had suffered from corruption scandals. In fact, an article in San Juan's largest newspaper, *El Nuevo Dia*, "charged that the seven years of the Rossello administration had witnessed the worst corruption in Puerto Rico in the past century."[24] The NPP nominated a close associate of the governor, Carlos Pesquera. However, he was defeated in the election by the PDP candidate, Sila Maria Calderón. She became the first elected female governor of the island.

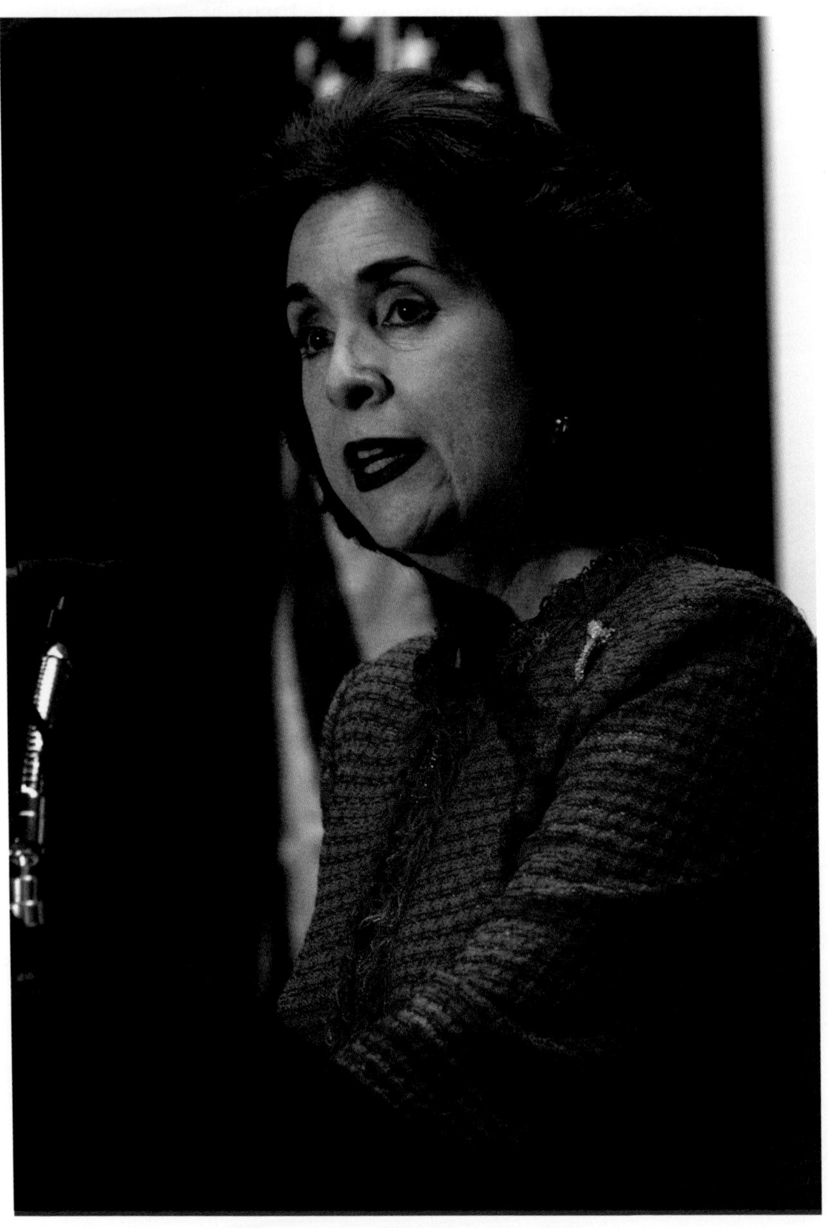

Puerto Rico Governor Sila Calderón

Corruption problems continued during Calderón's administration. A poll was conducted in 2004, in which a majority of people said that "political corruption has never been worse than under the present PPD [PDP] administration, led by Sila Maria Calderón."[25]

Calderón did not run for reelection. The PDP candidate was Anibal Acevedo Vila. In a close vote, he was elected the new governor in 2004. He had previously served as the Puerto Rican resident commissioner in Washington. The new governor focused on improving the commonwealth status of the island. He also committed himself to improving the economy. Economic conditions in Puerto Rico were affected by a change in US tax laws. In 2005 American businesses operating in Puerto Rico had to begin paying corporate income taxes. According to one report, "Preferential tax treatment for multinational companies was a major factor in attracting pharmaceutical and electronics firms to set up subsidiaries [offices] there..." As a result, the Puerto Rican economy was expected to continue struggling.[26] Indeed, a report issued in late 2006 said that poverty was still a major problem. Puerto Ricans earned only half of what people earned in the poorest state in the United States.

Leaving the Island

Many Puerto Ricans had long since given up on the island's economy. By the late 1950s, four hundred thousand islanders had left Puerto Rico for the United States' eastern seaboard.[27] They were not considered immigrants since they were American citizens under Puerto Rico's commonwealth status. They were lured by jobs in manufacturing and agriculture. Many Puerto Rican migrants settled in

Puerto Rican Pride

The National Puerto Rican Day Parade is a tradition that dates back to 1958. The parade is a celebration of all inhabitants of Puerto Rico as well as those with Puerto Rican heritage now living in the United States.

Every year, the parade takes place on Fifth Avenue in New York City on the second Sunday in June. Tens of thousands participate and millions more line the streets to enjoy the sights and sounds of the parade. It is an opportunity for Puerto Ricans to demonstrate their pride in their culture and history through costumes, music, and dance.

cities. These included New York; Hartford, Connecticut; and Boston.

Wages were higher in the United States, but the cost of living was also more expensive. Puerto Ricans often struggled with poverty. Many migrants also spoke little English and had little education. As a result, they were often forced to take low-paying jobs. They also faced prejudice from white Americans.

Migration continued into the first part of the twenty-first century. Education in Puerto Rico had improved. This meant that more and more migrants were arriving in the United States with college educations. As a result, they qualified for higher-paying jobs. Instead of heading for New York, they went to other cities, like Chicago and Los

The Puerto Rican Day parade in New York City draws a huge crowd every year.

Angeles. Meanwhile, many migrants had put down roots in the United States. Their children learned to speak English. They graduated from high school, attended college, and began enjoying a better standard of living than their parents did.

The population of Puerto Ricans in the United States had reached approximately 3.5 million by 2006. Many of them were born in the continental United States. But they often retained strong ties with Puerto Rico. Many Puerto Ricans who lived on the American mainland stayed in close touch with relatives on the island. In addition, Puerto Rican migrants left the United States mainland to return to Puerto Rico each year. They regarded themselves as Puerto Ricans. They had a separate culture and lifestyle—a unique island home.

For Puerto Ricans returning to the island, one of the most burning issues was the future status of Puerto Rico. That issue was highlighted late in 2005. In September, Filiberto Ojeda Rios was killed in a shoot-out with the American FBI. Ojeda Rios was a member of Los Macheteros. He was wanted in connection with a bank robbery in 1983. According to one report, Ojeda Rios "had been a leading figure in the fight for Puerto Rican independence and against US colonial rule."[28]

Only a small number of Puerto Ricans supported independence. Nevertheless, the death of Ojeda Rios focused attention on the future of the island and its status.

Looking Toward the Future

Beginning in 2008, a new issue overwhelmed the island. The United States suffered a severe economic downturn that also affected much of the rest of the world. Some of the worst conditions could be found in Puerto Rico, where unemployment reached over 15 percent in 2014, higher than any part of the US mainland.[29] Stores closed across the island because consumers had little money to spend, and crime increased. As a result, an increasing number of people migrated to the mainland United States looking for work and greater security. On the island, the population declined by over 100,000, to 3.67 million.[30] Over a third of those who remained received food stamps to help them feed their families. This is higher than any state on the mainland. At the same time, the government of Puerto Rico was $70 billion in debt, with no way to pay off the American banks that had loaned the island money.[31]

In 2012, while Puerto Rico continued to grapple with this crisis, people went to the polls to vote on two important issues. One of these was the selection of the next governor. Luis Fortuno, the incumbent and leader of the New Progressive Party, was running against Alejandro García Padilla, a member of the Popular Democratic Party. In a tightly contested election, Padilla was elected with a razor thin margin of less than 12,000 votes out of about 1.8 million cast in the election.[32]

Also on the ballot was a question on the future status of the island. Voters were asked to decide if they were happy with the present status of Puerto Rico as a commonwealth and, if not, whether they wanted the island to become a state. One voter, Jerome Lefebre, said "Puerto Rico has to be a state. We're doing OK but we could do better. We would receive more benefits, a lot more financial help (from Washington)." Ramon Lopez de Azua disagreed. "Puerto Rico's problem is not political status," he said. "I think that the United States is the best country in the world but I am Puerto Rican first."[33]

Demonstrators march in support of statehood for Puerto Rico.

According to the ballot returns, about 54 percent of the voters said that they were not happy with the current status, and about 61 percent of those said that Puerto Rico should become a state. The US Congress and President Obama had to decide whether to begin the process leading to statehood.[34] Interestingly, Fortuna had supported statehood, while Padilla supports the current status of the Puerto Rican commonwealth.

In 2015 the island was still debating this issue while also battling an economic downturn and teetering on the brink of bankruptcy. During his first two years in office, Governor Padilla reduced the size of the Puerto Rican budget deficit, while he began improving the economy and adding more jobs. This latest crisis was not unlike the many challenges that the island of Puerto Rico had experienced in the past. Nevertheless, its people have a strong culture and a rich history that will continue to influence the continental United States.

TRANSITO
PARE

TIMELINE

1493 Christoper Columbus lands on Puerto Rico.

1508 Ponce de León establishes a colony on Puerto Rico.

1511 Taíno Indians stage an unsuccessful revolt against Spanish.

1529 Carib Indians attack Puerto Rico.

1530 Severe hurricanes strike Puerto Rico.

1540 Spanish fortify San Juan.

1595 British attack Puerto Rico and are driven off by Spanish.

1625 Dutch attack Puerto Rico.

1765 First census taken of settlers on Puerto Rico.

1797 British attack Puerto Rico and are defeated by Spanish.

1820s Spain loses colonies in Latin America due to revolts; Puerto Rico remains part of empire.

1826 Slave code is developed to govern treatment of slaves in Puerto Rico.

1847 Spanish issue libreta law to control jornaleros.

1850s Laws passed to restrict freedom of Creoles.

1868 El Grito de Lares rebellion breaks out against Spanish rule.

1870 Colonists are permitted to form political parties.

1897 Puerto Ricans achieve autonomy from Spain.

1898	Spanish-American War breaks out; Puerto Rico becomes part of United States.
1900	Foraker Act is passed to govern Puerto Rico.
1910	Luis Muñoz Rivera becomes resident commissioner from Puerto Rico to the United States.
1917	Jones Act replaces Foraker Act.
1940s	Operation Bootstrap begins to improve economy.
1948	Luis Muñoz Marin becomes first elected governor of Puerto Rico.
1952	Puerto Rico becomes a commonwealth.
1970s	Food stamps are introduced in Puerto Rico.
1996	Young Bill introduced; Puerto Ricans confirm commonwealth status.
2000	Sila Maria Calderón becomes first elected female governor.
2004	Anibal Acevedo Vila becomes governor.
2008	Serious recession grips Puerto Rico.
2012	Puerto Ricans vote on island's status; majority vote for statehood.
2014	Puerto Rican government nears bankruptcy.

CHAPTER NOTES

Chapter 1. The Lares Uprising

1. Olga Jiménez de Wagenheim, *Puerto Rico's Revolt for Independence: El Grito de Lares* (Princeton, N.J.: Marcus Wiener Publishing, 1993), 58–59.
2. Ibid., 39.
3. Ibid., 46.
4. Ibid., 86–87.
5. Ibid., 101.

Chapter 2. A Conflict of Cultures

1. R. A. Van Middeldyk, *The History of Puerto Rico* (CreateSpace Independent Publishing Platform, 2013), 11.
2. Olga Jiménez de Wagenheim, *Puerto Rico: An Interpretive History from Pre-Columbian Times to 1900* (1998, repr., Princeton, N.J.: Markus Wiener Publishers, 2014), 15.
3. Middeldyk, 13.
4. Karl Wagenheim and Olga de Wagenheim, eds., *The Puerto Ricans: A Documentary History* (Princeton, N.J.: Markus Wiener Publishers, 2013), 19.
5. Middeldyk, 13.
6. Wagenheim, *Puerto Rico*, 43.
7. Middeldyk, 17.
8. Wagenheim, *Puerto Rico*, 46.
9. Middeldyk, 58.

Chapter 3. The Spanish Government

1. Olga Jiménez de Wagenheim, *Puerto Rico: An Interpretive History from Pre-Columbian Times to 1900* (1998, repr., Princeton, N.J.: Markus Wiener Publishers, 2014), 50.
2. R. A. Van Middeldyk, *The History of Puerto Rico* (New York: D. Appleton, 2013), 40–41.
3. Ibid., 37.
4. Ibid., 44.
5. Wagenheim, *Puerto Rico*, 56.
6. Ibid., 50–51.

7. Arturo Morales Carrion, *Puerto Rico: A Political and Cultural History* (New York: W.W. Norton, 1983), 34–35.
8. Ibid., 35.
9. Ibid., 37.
10. Ibid.
11. Wagenheim, *Puerto Rico*, 72.
12. Carrion, 10.
13. Ibid., 21.
14. Wagenheim, *Puerto Rico*, 73.
15. Carrion, 20.
16. Wagenheim, *Puerto Rico*, 74.

Chapter 4. Colonial Growth and Development

1. James Dietz, *Economic History of Puerto Rico* (Princeton, N.J.: Princeton University Press, 1986), 10–11.
2. Karl Wagenheim and Olga de Wagenheim, eds., *The Puerto Ricans: A Documentary History* (Princeton, N.J: Markus Wiener Publishers, 2013), 36.
3. Olga Jiménez de Wagenheim, *Puerto Rico: An Interpretive History from Pre-Columbian Times to 1900* (1998, repr., Princeton, N.J.: Markus Wiener Publishers, 2014), 88.
4. Wagenheim and Wagenheim, 40.
5. Dietz, 36.
6. Wagenheim, *Puerto Rico*, 91.
7. Ibid., 109.
8. Olga Jiménez de Wagenheim, *Puerto Rico's Revolt for Independence: El Grito de Lares* (Princeton, N.J.: Markus Wiener Publishing, 1993), 5.
9. Wagenheim, *Puerto Rico*, 118.
10. Ibid., 133.
11. Dietz, 37.
12. Wagenheim and Wagenheim, 57–58.
13. Dietz, 70.
14. Ibid., 44.
15. Wagenheim, *Puerto Rico's Revolt for Independence*, 21.
16. Ibid., 23.
17. Ibid., 13.

Chapter 5. The Spanish-American War

1. James Dietz, *Economic History of Puerto Rico* (Princeton, N.J.: Princeton University Press, 1986), 75.
2. José Trias Monge, *Puerto Rico: The Trials of the Oldest Colony in the World* (New Haven, Conn.: Yale University Press, 1997), 12.
3. Ibid., 22.
4. Ibid., 23.
5. Ibid., 24.
6. Olga Jiménez de Wagenheim, *Puerto Rico: An Interpretive History from Pre-Columbian Times to 1900* (1998, repr., Princeton, N.J.: Markus Wiener Publishers, 2014), 197.
7. Ibid., 200.
8. Arturo Morales Carrion, *Puerto Rico: A Political and Cultural History* (New York: W.W. Norton, 1983), 132.
9. Ibid., 133.
10. Wagenheim, *Puerto Rico*, 206.

Chapter 6. Puerto Rico Changes Direction

1. Karl Wagenheim and Olga de Wagenheim, eds., *The Puerto Ricans: A Documentary History* (Princeton, N.J.: Markus Wiener Publishers, 2013), 109.
2. Pedro Caban, *Constructing a Colonial People: Puerto Rico and the United States, 1898–1932* (Boulder, Colo.: Westview Press, 1999), 51.
3. José Trias Monge, *Puerto Rico: The Trials of the Oldest Colony in the World* (New Haven, Conn.: Yale University Press, 1997), 33.
4. Caban, 55.
5. James Dietz, *Economic History of Puerto Rico* (Princeton, N.J.: Princeton University Press, 1986), 84.
6. Monge, 52.
7. Dietz, 94.
8. Monge, 57.
9. Dietz, 99–100.
10. Ibid., 108–109.
11. César J. Ayala, *American Sugar Kingdom: The Political Economy of the Spanish Caribbean, 1898–1934* (Chapel Hill, N.C.: University of North Carolina Press, 1999), 139.

12. Dietz, 111.
13. Ibid., 117.
14. Monge, 61.
15. Ibid., 64.
16. Ibid., 73.
17. Dietz, 128.
18. Wagenheim and Wagenheim, 183.
19. Dietz, 137–139; Monge, 83; *A Documentary History*, 166.
20. Monge, 97.
21. Dietz, 179.

Chapter 7. Self-Government for Puerto Rico

1. Ronald Fernandez, *The Disenchanted Island: Puerto Rico and the Unites States in the Twentieth Century* (Westport, Conn.: Praeger, 1996), 179.
2. Ibid., 180.
3. Ibid., 185.
4. Ibid., 182.
5. José Trias Monge, *Puerto Rico: The Trials of the Oldest Colony in the World* (New Haven, Conn.: Yale University Press, 1997), 119.
6. James Dietz, *Economic History of Puerto Rico* (Princeton, N.J.: Princeton University Press, 1986), 237.
7. Fernandez, 193.
8. Monge, 130.
9. Dietz, 244.
10. Ibid., 248.
11. Ibid., 274.
12. Ibid., 275.
13. Fernandez, 230.
14. Ibid.
15. Dietz, 299.
16. Fernandez, 249.
17. Monge, 160.
18. Terry Baynes, "U.S. court dismisses Puerto Ricans' suit over arms tests," February 14, 2012, www.reuters.com/article/2012/02/15/us-puertorico-lawsuit-vieques-idUSTRE81E07Y20120215.
19. Fernandez, 261.

20. Ruben Berrios Martinez, "Puerto Rico's Decolonization," *Foreign Affairs*, November/December, 1997.
21. Ralph de Toledano, "Does Puerto Rico Deserve Independence?," June 3, 2002, 48.
22. "Puerto Rico's Stalemate," *The Christian Science Monitor*, December 18, 1998, 10.
23. *The World Factbook: Puerto Rico* (Washington, D.C.: The Central Intelligence Agency, 2006), 453.
24. Economist Intelligence Unit, "Political Scene: Issue of Corruption Becomes an Election Focus," *Country Report Puerto Rico April 2000*, April 17, 2000.
25. Economist Intelligence Unit, "Puerto Rico Politics: Coming Gubernatorial Vote Still Uncertain," *Country Briefing 2004*, July 26, 2004.
26. Economist Intelligence Unit, "Outlook for 2005–2006: Inter-6ational Relations," *Country Report Puerto Rico July 2005*, July 6, 2005.
27. Fernandez, 192.
28. "FBI Assassinates Puerto Rican Nationalist Leader Filiberto 8jeda Rios," September 26, 2005, http://www. democracynow.org/article.pl?sid=05/09/26/14342297, December 2, 2006.
29. Lizette Alvarez, "Economy and Crime Spur New Puerto Rican Exodus," *The New York Times*, February 8, 2014, www.nytimes.com/2014/02/09/us/economy-and-crime-spur-new-puerto-rican-exodus.html.
30. "Puerto Rico Population," *Trading Economics*, accessed January 9, 2015, www.tradingeconomics.com/puerto-rico/population.
31. Alvarez.
32. Puerto Rico Report, "Deciphering Puerto Rico's Election Results," November 11, 2012, www.puertoricoreport.com/deciphering-puerto-ricos-election-results/.
33. "Election 2012: Puerto Rico Votes on U.S. Ties and Chooses Governor," November 6, 2012, bigstory.ap.org/article/puerto-rico-votes-on-us-ties-and-chooses-governor-0.
34. Cristina Constantini and Jordan Fabian, "Puerto Ricans Send Strong Message They Favor Statehood in Tight Elections," November 11, 2012, abcnews.go.com/ABC_Univision/Politics/puerto-ricans-vote-statehood-oust-pro-statehood-governor/story?id=17660813.

GLOSSARY

agregados—Squatters who lived on farmland without permission.

arquebus—Early rifle used by soldiers in the sixteenth century.

bohio—A small, round hut built by the Taíno Indians.

cabildo—Spanish town government.

cacique—A chief of the Taíno Indians.

Creoles—White Hispanic settlers born in Puerto Rico.

Provincial Deputation—Advisors to the governor of Puerto Rico.

encomienda—Spanish farm in the New World.

guarda costas—Sea captains who guarded the coast of Puerto Rico.

hacendado—Owner of a large farm.

hacienda—Large farm.

intendant—Official in charge of financial affairs.

jibaros—Peasant farmers.

jornaleros—Hired workers on a large farm.

libreta—A workbook carried by a hired worker with his days worked.

peninsulares—Spanish immigrants to Puerto Rico.

plebiscite—A vote by the people of a country to decide on an issue.

regidores—Officials who ran the cabildos.

repartimiento—Distribution of Taíno Indians to work on Spanish farms.

situado—Special fund to finance government expenses.

FURTHER READING

Books

Arkham, Thomas. *Both Puerto Rican and American.* Broomall, Pa.: Mason Crest, 2012.

Bjorklund, Ruth. *Puerto Rico.* New York: Benchmark Books, 2013.

Carlisle, Rodney P. *The Hispanic Americans.* New York: Facts on File, 2011.

Gagne, Tammy. *Caribbean Cultures in Perspective.* Hockessin, Del.: Mitchell Lane, 2014.

Stille, Darlene. *Puerto Rico.* Danbury, Conn.: Children's Press, 2014.

Web Sites

everyculture.com/No-Sa/Puerto-Rico.html

Covers the history, language, culture, and politics of Puerto Rico.

nps.gov/nr/twhp/wwwlps/lessons/60sanjuan/60sanjuan.htm

Explains the history of Puerto Rico's defensive system through maps, pictures, readings, and activities.

loc.gov/rr/hispanic/1898/puertorico.html

Provides a detailed look at the Spanish-American War.

INDEX